by S. J. PERELMAN

The Ill-Tempered Clavichord

By S. J. PERELMAN

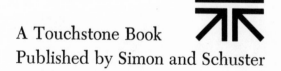

A Touchstone Book
Published by Simon and Schuster

A Touchstone Book
Published by Simon and Schuster
Rockefeller Center, 630 Fifth Avenue
New York, New York 10020

First paperback printing 1971
SBN 671-20900-0 Touchstone paperback edition
Manufactured in the United States of America

Except for "Young as You Feel," all the
articles in this book appeared originally in
The New Yorker. That chapter appeared
originally in *Redbook*.

TO *G. S. Lobrano*

Contents

Contents

The Ill-Tempered Clavichord

Up the Close and
down the Stair

I'M NO BLOODY HERO, and when the Princess Pats stood at
Passchendaele in '17, I was damned careful to be twelve
years old and three thousand miles to the rear, selling
Domes of Silence after school to the housewives of Cres-
cent Park, Rhode Island. I never go out of my way to
borrow trouble, but if it comes, I pride myself I can face
up to it as well as the average Johnny. I once spent a night
in a third-class carriage in the F.M.S. with seventy-odd
indentured Chinese out of Swatow and Amoy bound up-
country for the tin mines at Ipoh. Blasted engine broke
a coupling, way up the back of beyond in Negri Sembilan,
and there we sat, rain pelting through the roof, not a cup

3

of tea to be had, and every mother's son of them smoking chandoo and tucking in rice mixed with *trassi,* compared to which even the durian is attar of roses. Worse luck, the coolie in the berth over mine kept munching bananas and dropping the skins on me; half a dozen times, you'd have sworn a cobra or a Russell's viper was loose in your bed. Touch and go, as they say, but I bit on the bullet and the old buckram carried me through. Another time, down Amboina way in the Moluccas, a chap buying *bêche-de-mer* and shell in the Kai and Aru groups southeast of Ceram offered me a lift as far as Banda Neira in his prahu. A filthy scow she was, thirty-five tons, with a poop deck and double sweeps, manned by a crew of Bugi who'd slip a kris into you at the drop of a diphthong. Well, you know the Banda Sea at the turn of the monsoon, treacherous as a woman, waves thirty feet high one minute and flat calm the next, wind howling like a thousand devils and sharks all over the ruddy place. Thinks I, weighing the beggar's proposal in the bar in Amboina, steady on, old son, better have another drink on it. We'd a second bottle of *genever* and a third, till I could almost feel the eyes start out of my blooming head. Lord knows how I managed to stick it, but she sailed without me and that was the last ever heard of the lot of them. I probably would have heard more, except I had to rush back to New York to see about my Social Security.

Yes, the going has to be pretty rugged before I show the white feather, and when it comes along, I'm willing to own up to it. A couple of weeks ago, business called me up to town from my Pennsylvania retreat and I stayed alone overnight at our flat in Greenwich Village. This much I'll say: I've knocked about a bit and I've taken the rough with the smooth, but I wouldn't duplicate that experience for all the rubies in the Shwe Dagon Pagoda. Just in a manner of speaking, that is. If anybody wants to talk a deal, I can be in Rangoon in two days.

Maybe, since the circumstances were special, I ought to sketch in the background. Last December, deferring to my wife's prejudice against sleeping on subway gratings, I moved the family into a handsome old brownstone on West Ninth Street. It was a charming house, its brick front weathered a soft rose under the ivy, with a cool, spacious stair well and a curving walnut balustrade worn smooth by the hands of many a defaulting tenant. Determined to apportion the charm among the greatest possible number of people, the owner had cut up the premises into eight apartments, and the top floors in particular into two minute duplexes, the rear one of which we invested. It commanded an unbroken view of a health-food shop on Eighth Street, and of a dismal winter afternoon it was heartening to watch the dyspeptics totter out carrying pails of blackstrap molasses and wheat germ, their faces exalted with the gospel of Gayelord Hauser. The services, to be candid, were deplorable. The hot-water taps supplied a brown viscous fluid similar to cocoa, the radiators beat an unending tomtom like the Royal Watusi Drums, and the refrigerator poached our food instead of chilling it, but the mem and I didn't care a fig. We were living

5

graciously; we could breathe. We thanked our lucky stars we weren't cooped up in one of those great uniform apartments on Park Avenue, full of stall showers and gas ranges that work, and all kinds of depressing gadgets.

About a month after moving in, I learned a beguiling fact from another tenant; viz., that three decades before, the house had been the scene of an audacious heist. To recap the affair briefly: One Sunday afternoon in April, 1922, Mr. and Mrs. Frederick Gorsline, the wealthy elderly couple who occupied the mansion, were enjoying a siesta when five yeggs, led by a French high-binder once employed there as relief butler, gained entrance. They overpowered the householders and their staff of eight, locked them in a wine vault in the basement, and fled, bearing gems and silver worth approximately eighty thousand dollars. That the prisoners escaped from the vault alive was due solely to the sangfroid and enterprise of its seventy-three-year-old owner; working in total darkness with a penknife and a ten-cent piece, he succeeded after two hours in loosening the screws that held the combination in place, and opened the door. He then expended seven years and a sizable part of his bundle tracking down the culprits, the last of whom, the ringleader, was apprehended in France and transported to Devil's Island.

I, naturally, lost no time in making a close scrutiny of the vault with a wax taper, or something the man at the hardware store assured me was a wax taper, and convinced myself of the veracity of the story. I even found a dime embedded in a crack in the floor; it was dated 1936, but I filed off the final numerals and worked up a rather effective account of my role in the case, which folks used to clamor for at our parties this past spring. It was funny the way they'd clamor for it, sometimes without even opening their mouths. They'd just stand there and sort of *yearn,* and being host, of course, I'd have to oblige. But all that is by the way. You're clamoring to hear about the night I put in alone there.

WELL, I got downtown about six of a Friday evening, pretty well bushed, no engagements on hand. (Curious the way they'd rather stay home and wash their hair than accept a date at the last minute. I never will understand it.) As I say, I was done up and looking forward to a quiet session with Gibbon or Trevelyan, eleven hours of shuteye, and an early start back to Pennsylvania in the morning. One of our neighbors, a young fellow who poses for those Bronzini neckwear ads of people with their torsos transfixed by a dirk, was loading a portable sewing machine and a nest of salad bowls into the back of his MG.

"Huddo," he said, startled. "I thought you-all had cleared out." I explained my presence and he shuddered. "Too ghastly. Everyone in the house is away. The Cadmuses drove off this minute to their haunt in Bucks. Even Benno Troglodeit's gone to the beach, and you know what an old stick-in-the-mud *he* is."

"Solitude don't make no never-mind to me," I said loftily. "When one's kicked around the far places of the earth as much as I have, he becomes pretty self-sufficient.

7

I recall one time in Trebizond—" The roar of his powerful little engine drowned out the remainder of my sentence, and with a flick of his wrist he was speeding down Ninth Street. Sensational acceleration, those MGs.

I watched him out of sight, then slowly went upstairs. Somehow—I couldn't have said why—a puzzling change of mood had overtaken me, a vague and indescribable malaise. The house, too, seemed to have altered mysteriously; the stair well was nowhere as cool or spacious as it had been in the past. The air smelled stagnant and oppressive, as though it had been filtered through hot plush, and I imagined some unspeakable secret behind each doorway I passed. Fumbling the key into the lock of our apartment, the distorted, waxen faces of Andrew and Abby Borden rose up before me; with a galvanic twitch, I flung open the door, darted inside, and bolted it fast. By the weak rays of light struggling through the drawn Venetian blinds, I took careful stock of the living room, its floor devoid of carpets and the furniture shrouded in dust covers. Nothing appeared amiss, but I decided to double-check. I licked my lips and spoke in a soft, placating tone that made it clear I wouldn't give offense to a dog. "Is anybody home?" I inquired. It goes without saying that had a reply been vouchsafed, I was prepared to drop dead instantly. Satisfied no corporeal intruders were astir, I stole on padded feet upstairs to the bedrooms—trekking through the jungles of southern Siam long ago taught me how to move without disturbing a twig—and made a routine tour of the closets.

Just as I was feeling around gingerly among the topcoats for any unauthorized bodies, the telephone gave a sudden, nerve-shattering peal. I sprang out and flattened myself against the wall near the instrument, every faculty tensed. Something very, very unsavory was afoot; I distinctly remembered having cancelled the service myself a month before. Ought I answer or play for time? Trying to envision the face at the other end, the twisted smile and the narrow, baleful eyes, I felt perspiration ooze from my scalp. Then equilibrium returned; better to know my enemy than succumb to this nameless, creeping horror. I picked up the receiver. "Grand Central Roach Control," I said tonelessly. "Leonard Vesey speaking." There was a watchful pause, and, realizing the full stature of his adversary, the unknown hung up discomfited.

The first round was mine, but from now on my only safety lay in extreme vigilance. With a view toward sharpening my sensibilities to razor edge, I decided to toss off two fingers of brandy neat. A search of the kitchen cupboards failed to elicit any such restorative; I did, however, turn up a can of warm tomato juice whose top I finally breached with an apple corer. Five or six gauze pads soon dried the trifling gash in my wrist, and, stripping down to my shorts (for I was not minded to carry excess poundage if an emergency arose), I opened my Gibbon to the campaigns of Diocletian.

How noble a spirit infuses those stately periods, what sapience and celestial calm! Musing on the paltriness of latter-day historians, I fell into a gentle reverie that must have lasted close to four hours.

SHORTLY after midnight, I came awake with the ineradicable conviction that I had neglected some vital obligation. I lay rigid, struggling to recapture it, and suddenly it flashed over me. In the hustle and bustle of moving last fall, I had forgotten to tip the janitor of our new quarters at Christmastime. Suppose, for argument's sake, that he had been brooding over the slight. Suppose that his bitterness had developed into a persecution mania that demanded my extinction, that he had seen me enter the house alone tonight, had seized the chance to put me out of the way, and, at this very moment, was tiptoeing stealthily up the stairs, cleaver in hand. I saw myself cruelly dismembered, my head in a hatbox as in "Night Must Fall," my extremities wrapped in burlap and dispersed through a dozen railway checkrooms. Tears of self-pity welled up in my eyes; I was too young to die in such meaningless fashion, victim of a madman's whim. What would become of my brood in Pennsylvania, waiting for the paternal hug and the sweetmeats that never came? I resolved to sell my life as dearly as possible. Grimly rolling up my figurative sleeves, I was about to burrow under the quilt when a muffled clang from below turned me to stone.

In that awful instant, all the details of the Gorsline robbery reverted with diamond clarity, and the whole hideous truth dawned on me. The police, despite their rodomontade, had never really regained the loot; the brains of the mob had hidden it somewhere in the building, and now, after twenty-nine years in the hell of French Guiana, had come back to exhume it and settle old scores. Like Jonathan Small in "The Sign of Four," returning to Pondicherry Lodge from the Andamans to claim the Agra Treasure, he was a beast unchained, and in slamming the door of the vault he was notifying the occupants of the house that their hour had struck. All that remained was the stab of the poisoned thorn and the last convulsive agony. Ten minutes hence, my features frozen in the dreadful *risus sardonicus,* I would be indistinguishable from Bartholomew Sholto. I was a gone coon.

And yet, such is the complexity of the human spirit, and especially one molded in the crucible of the East, not a muscle flickered in my lean cheek. Instead, I was filled with a vast, consuming anger; I was determined to invade the vault and purge society of this loathsome scourge if it meant annihilation. I routed out the wax taper, boldly flung open the door, and descended the stairs with catlike tread. Just as I neared the first-floor landing, a feminine voice, taut with a terrible urgency, drifted up to me from below.

"Put your back into it," it was saying harshly. "We've got to crack it tonight, I tell you." I repressed an involuntary snort of triumph. So that was it; a woman was mixed up in it—indubitably had engineered the entire caper, as I had suspected from the beginning. Pressed close to the balustrade, I worked myself down along it with infinite caution and peered around the stairhead.

The sight that met my eyes was one calculated to unsettle the most magnificent aplomb. Clad in a flowered kimono that ill concealed her generous charms, Mrs. Purdy Woolwine, the first-floor tenant, knelt by a galvanized rubbish can, striving to anchor it to the floor. Her gleaming coiffure was disordered and her face contorted like that of a wrestler in a Japanese print. At her side, a small, sallow man, whom I dimly recognized as Woolwine, had driven a screwdriver under the lid with the aid of a hammer and was desperately trying to prise it off, obviously bent on disposing of a wastebasket heaped high with bottles and fruit rinds. Neither of them was aware of my existence, nor would they ever have discovered it but for an unbearable compulsion to sneeze. As my wild "Kerchow!" rang out, they wheeled convulsively and beheld me, bone-naked in my shorts and taper in hand, agape on the landing. With an eerie screech that shook the Piranesi reproductions off the walls, Mrs. Woolwine half rose and toppled sidewise in a dead faint.

FANTASTIC how people deliberately misconstrue the most innocent occurrence. Damn my eyes if I wasn't two hours explaining away the affair to those chuckleheads from the Eighth Precinct. They'd got the wind up, don't you see, had to find a scapegoat and all that frightful rot. You'd have thought I was Harvey Hawley Crippen, the way they mucked about with their sobriety tests and their argel-bargel about Peeping Toms and God knows what all. Ah, well, it's over and done with now, thank goodness. I spend most of my time these days down in Pennsylvania, and, come autumn, we'll probably find digs more suited to the family needs. Might even go out East again, between you and me. I've had my fill of gracious living and cocktail kit-kit and hysteroids named Mrs. Purdy Woolwine. I breathe better in some place like Amboina, where nobody asks any questions, where all you need is a twist of cotton around your loins and a pinch of rice, and a man's past is his own.

Nesselrode to Jeopardy

"The sauce is loaded with dynamite when carelessly prepared," a Health Department spokesman declared yesterday. "It has become one of the bureau's worst headaches. . . ."

Many temperamental chefs, it was learned, resent the Health Department's infringement on their culinary art. One chef, for example, refused to tell an inspector how he made the sauce because it was a "secret technique" that he had learned in France.

Several weeks later, five persons contracted food poisoning at the restaurant because of the hollandaise. The Health Department then demanded to know the chef's secret and found that his technique consisted of straining the sauce through a cheesecloth bag that must be squeezed with the hands.—*The Times.*

WHENEVER I turn over the whole grotesque affair in my mind, trying to rationalize the baffling complex of events that overtook me on the French Riviera this autumn, I always ask myself the same questions. What would have happened if Destiny, unpredictable jade, had drawn my laggard feet to some hotel other than the Villa Heliotrope? What if Anglo-Saxon shyness had sealed Colin Rentschler's lips and he had not impulsively come to the aid of a fellow-American in hazard? Would I ever have met that elegant assassin, Colonel Firdausi of the Turkish secret police, or cowered in the hold of a rusty Greek steamer bound for the Piraeus, or given chase at midnight to a music-hall juggler over the roofs of Montparnasse? In short, why should I, timid recluse, have been wantonly singled out for a supporting role in a nightmare as fantastic as the riddle of the cheesecloth bag, a problem to shame the wildest conceits of an Eric Ambler or a Carol Reed? And why—except that it is highly traditional—do I ask these questions all over again when I should be getting on with my story?

To begin at the beginning, I'd been down at Fez, in North Africa, all summer, working on a book of favorite recipes of famous people like Tennessee Williams, Paul Bowles, Truman Capote, and Speed Lamkin, and my nerves were at sixes and sevens. I felt completely drained, used up; I'd pretty well exhausted my emotional bank balance doing the necessary research, and I knew it was touch and go unless I immured myself in some quiet pied-à-terre where I could slough off superficialities and organize my material. I shan't burden you with tedious autobiographical details, but perhaps I ought to explain that my people (poor bourgeois dears) left me a goodish bit of money. Praise be to Allah—and the automobile wax my father invented—I don't have to fret excessively about the sordid aspects of life, and hence I've applied myself to living graciously, which I do think is all that matters, really. I mean I sometimes wonder if a properly chilled Gibson or a superb *coq au vin* isn't basically more important than these grubby wars and revolutions everyone's being so hopelessly neurotic about. Not that money's actually vital to my existence, mind you; one art I've mastered is how to make do with the absolute minimum. Given fair seats at the ballet, half a dozen friends with country houses from whom I can scrounge weekends, a few custom-tailored suits, some decent hand-lasted shoes —it's weakness, I know, but I'm fixated on good leather— and three months a year at Montreux or Bordighera, and I can live in a hole in the wall at the Crillon and rub along on a gigot and a crisp salad.

ANYHOW, I'd finally fetched up at the Villa Heliotrope, a modest little establishment on the Estérel coast west of Cannes, and everything was proving utterly ideal. The cuisine wasn't too repugnant, and if *Madame la Patronne* occasionally used overmuch musk on her embonpoint, she at least rationed it in her seasoning. Well, one evening I came in to dinner with a truly pagan appetite. (Ardent sun-worshipper that I am, I'd spent the entire day on the *plage*, baking a glorious golden brown.) I had just dispatched Madame's creditable *rôti* and was attacking the dessert when the chap at the next table cleared his throat.

"Easy does it," he said abruptly. "I wouldn't bolt that Nesselrode if I were you."

"Why the devil not?" I snapped, glaring around at him. Bolting's sort of a sacrament with me, I suppose, and I didn't much fancy the highhanded line he'd taken.

"Because it's lumpy," he said. "They forgot to strain it." I tasted a soupçon and found he was right. I turned back for another look at my neighbor. His lean, dark face showed good bone structure, and there was something about his trench coat and the gravy on his hat that bespoke the inspector of a metropolitan health department.

"Look here," I said, mystified. "You knew that pudding was lumpy?"

"It's my business to know things like that, friend," he said with an opaque smile. As he rose and passed me, a card fluttered down beside my plate. It bore the legend "Colin Rentschler," and, below, "Inspector, New York Health Department." I was pretty thoughtful the rest of the meal. Something curious was shaping up, and while I'm not especially intuitive, I felt Colin Rentschler might have some connection with it.

I was seated on the terrace that evening, sipping a final pousse-café before turning in, when his loose-jointed figure settled into the adjoining chair. After a rather watchful silence, he made some inconsequential remark about

17

the écru-colored sky's portending the advent of the mistral, the dry northerly wind characteristic of Provence. "Odd écru-colored sky, that," he observed. "Shouldn't wonder if it portends the advent of the mistral, the dry northerly wind characteristic of Provence."

"Yes," I agreed. "Sinister shade, isn't it? It reminds me of—well, of hollandaise sauce that's gone a trifle bad."

I heard the sharp, sudden intake of his breath, followed by a little click as he expelled it. When he spoke again, it was in a tight, strangled whisper that put shudders up my spine. "Then you know," he said. He glanced quickly over his shoulder and leaned forward, his eyes merciless as snails. "Listen. Pierre Moustique has been seen in Istanbul."

"Good God!" I murmured. Like everyone else, of course, I knew that New York gourmets were in a grip of terror due to a wave of hollandaise poisoning, and that Moustique, the chef who had betrayed his secret technique of squeezing the sauce through a cheesecloth bag with his bare hands, had escaped to Canada in a hamper of towels, but in the shimmering heat of Morocco I had lost touch with later developments, and my allusion to the evening sky had been made in all innocence. Before I could extricate myself, nonetheless, Fate, in the guise of a health inspector, had altered my future with a single decisive stroke.

"It's incredible"—Rentschler shrugged—"but then so is life. Last Thursday afternoon, Anna Popescu, a Moldavian seamstress in the Kadikoy quarter of Istanbul bearing a Nansen passport, reported that a chef closely resembling

Moustique had approached her to repair a rent in a cheesecloth bag, offering ninety piastres. When she hesitated, he fled." His harsh voice stabbed at me, insistent as the cicadas in the Mediterranean night. "Schneider, until we can lay Moustique by the heels and analyze that bag which its poisoned meshes spell finis for unwary epicures, death will lurk in every frond of broccoli. I have two tickets on the morning plane for Istanbul. Are you the man to share a desperate adventure?"

I picked up my glass and, twirling the stem meditatively, swallowed it in a single gulp. A mad, foolhardy errand, I thought, and still the challenge to gamble for consummate stakes awoke a tocsin in my blood. I spat out a spicule of glass, arose, and extended my hand. "Done and done, Rentschler," I said coolly. "I've always taken my liquor mixed and my peril neat, and I see no reason to switch now. Next stop, the Golden Horn!"

COLONEL FIRDAUSI, deputy director of the Turkish secret police, hoisted a polished cordovan boot to the edge of his desk and, extracting the monocle from his eye, carefully scraped a bit of *shish kebab* from the sole. As he dusted his delicate, saurian hands with a handkerchief strongly redolent of attar of roses, motes of halvah danced in the slanting beam of sunlight above his head.

"This is a very interesting tale you tell me, gentlemen," he said with a smile. Colonel Firdausi's smile could have refrigerated a whole chain of Turkish frozen-food stores.

"But I do not see precisely why you come to me. Surely you do not imply Pierre Moustique is still in Istanbul?"

"I imply that and more." Rentschler's left forefinger traced what was seemingly an idle pattern on the dusty arm of his chair, and then I realized with a start that he was scribbling a message to me. "Watch this man's mouth," it read, in Italian. "It is willful, sensual, that of a sybarite who will not cavil at resorting to violence if he is bilked." My colleague chuckled thinly, his steady gaze meeting Firdausi's square. "I imply, my dear Colonel, that he is in this selfsame room at the moment."

"You cease to amuse me, Monsieur." The Turkish official rapped the bell before him peremptorily. "The interview is ended. My secretary—"

"One second," cut in Rentschler. "Have you ever heard of the Club Libido, in Pera? No? Allow me to refresh your memory. The principal chanteuse at the Libido is Marie Farkas, a naturalized Transylvanian travelling under a League of Nations passport."

"Neither you nor Marie could possibly hope to surprise me," returned Firdausi icily. "I have been sleeping with the lady fifteen years."

"And therefore enjoy considerable seniority over me," admitted Rentschler. "Nevertheless, she has been fickle enough to confide that on your last two nuptial flights you wore a chef's cap, with the name of Pierre Moustique inscribed on the headband in indelible pencil."

"Inconstancy, thy name is woman," reflected Firdausi. "Ah, well, there is no use dissembling with such adversaries." Reaching into his tunic, he withdrew a green cheesecloth bag and tossed it pettishly on the blotter. "Is this what you are looking for?" As Rentschler's hand shot forward, it struck the ice-blue barrel of the Colonel's automatic. "Tchk, tchk, impetuous boy," chided Firdausi. "Be so good, both of you, as to lace your fingers over your heads. Thank you. Now, Messieurs, exposition is wearisome, so I will be succinct."

"I will be succincter," Rentschler put in. "The real Colonel Firdausi is reposing at this instant in the Bosporus, in a burlap sack weighted with stale nougat. You are about to bind us back to back in a similar pouch and deposit us alongside him, as a warning to meddlers not to interfere in matters that do not concern them. Need I point out, though, Moustique, that you cannot possibly hope to get away with it?"

"Of course not," agreed the other, withdrawing from his tunic a capacious burlap sack. "Still, in the brisk interplay of Near Eastern intrigue, these little—ah—involutions are mandatory. *Au 'voir,* gentlemen."

Forty-five minutes later, trussed up in the sack, we were jolting in a dray over the cobblestones fringing the waterside. Despite our extreme discomfort and the danger confronting us, however, my companion exhibited no hint of the disquiet that pervaded me. Listening to his tranquil comparison of the respective merits of the pickles obtainable at Lindy's and the Russian Tea Room, one might easily have imagined him in his own club. At length, my endurance crumbled.

"Dash it all, man!" I burst forth. "Here's one pickle your precious department won't get us out of!"

"No, but Victor Hugo will," he said evenly. "I take it you've read 'Les Misérables'?"

"This is hardly the time for a literary quiz," I interjected.

"You will recall," said Rentschler imperturbably, "that at an equally crucial pass Jean Valjean confounded Papa Thenardier and his gang by sawing through his bonds with a watch spring concealed in a penny. Tug manfully at your wrists." I complied, and, to my stupefaction, found myself liberated. The next thing I knew, Rentschler and I were racing through a maze of warehouses and cranes; I remember a ship's gangway clangorous with roustabouts shifting cargo, a lightning descent into a labyrinth of hatches, and, over the bellow of the siren, my colleague's unruffled explanation that we were stowaways aboard the *Thessalonian Schizophrene,* bound for the Piraeus and Trieste. Actually, we never went to either; a few hours later, Rentschler nudged me and we stole back on land. The whole thing had been a clever feint, for, as he pointed out, nobody was chasing us and there was no reason to slip out of the country illicitly. That night, seated in the aircraft droning toward London, I dully wondered what fresh complications lay in wait for us. But Fate and the stewardess, a shapely Philadelphian named Dougherty travelling under a nylon bust support, gave me back only an inscrutable smile.

THIN FINGERS of fog drifted across the West India Dock Road, tracing an eerie filigree across the street lamp under which Rentschler and I stood shivering in our mackintoshes. From time to time, almond-eyed devotees of the poppy, furtively hugging poppy-seed rolls, slid past us in their bast shoes, bent on heaven knows what baleful missions. For more than three hours, we had been breathlessly watching the draper's shop across the way, and I still had no clue as to why. Rentschler, shrewd judge of human foibles that he was, must have sensed my perplexity, for at last he broke silence.

"In the split second you saw that bag of Moustique's, Schneider," he queried, "did any thought occur to you?"

"Why, yes," I said, surprised. "I remember thinking there was only one shop in Europe that handles cheesecloth of that type—Arthur Maggot's Sons, in the West India Dock Road. But I still can't fathom why we've spent three hours casing it."

"No particular reason," he rejoined. "It's just the kind of patient, plodding labor the public never gives one credit for in this profession. Come on, let's move in."

Bartholomew Maggot shrugged his vulpine shoulders irascibly and, applying a pinch of Copenhagen snuff to his nostril, opened the cash register and sneezed into it. A half hour's questioning had merely aggravated his normally waspish temper, and it was dishearteningly plain that we had reached an impasse. Rentschler, notwithstanding, refused to yield.

"This man who asked you to appraise his cheesecloth bag yesterday," he persisted. "You say he was hooded and smelled of attar of roses, but surely you must have noticed something unusual about him."

"No, sir, I did not," growled the draper. "Wait a bit, though, there *was* something. His lapel had a few grains of rice powder on it—the sort those French music-hall artistes wear."

"You've a sharp pair of eyes in your head, Maggot," complimented the inspector. "It's a pity we don't know where they came from."

"Why, this one came from Harrod's," explained Maggot, removing it. "It's glass, as you see, and has a little Union Jack in it. The other—"

"No, no, the grains," Rentschler interrupted testily. "Haven't you any idea which music-hall uses that type of powder?"

"Let me see," said Maggot slowly. "The cove was carrying a theatrical valise with the name of Pierre Moustique, Bobino Theatre, Rue de la Gaité, Paris, France, painted on it in white letters, but I didn't really pay much mind."

"Humph," muttered Rentschler. His quick, deductive mind had caught something of importance in the other's words. "A very good evening to you, Mr. Maggot, and now, Schneider, to Paris *en grand vitesse*. Are you hungry? I think I can promise a ragout spiced with melodrama and served piping hot." I have often thought the world lost a major poet when Colin Rentschler joined the New York Health Department.

THE MINGLED SCENT of caporal, cheap perfume, and garlic hung like a pall over the motley audience jamming the stalls of the Bobino, the Left Bank's most popular vaudeville. A succession of weight-lifters, trained dogs, diseuses, and trick cyclists had displayed their enchantments, and now, as the curtain rose on the final turn and M. l'Inconnu, the masked juggler, strode into the glare of the footlights, my heart began beating like a trip hammer. Those delicate, saurian hands, the heavy odor of attar of roses—I racked my memory vainly, trying to recollect where I had met them before. A buzz of excited speculation rose from the patrons surrounding us; rumor ran rife that l'Inconnu was an unfrocked chef from New York, a quondam Turkish police official, a recent arrival from Limehouse, but none knew for sure. Yet some sixth sense told me that Rentschler, his hawk's profile taut in the darkness beside me, was close to the answer.

"*Messieurs et dames!*" The guttural voice of Pierre Moustique suddenly set my every nerve atingle. "I now attempt a feat to dizzy the imagination, keeping *trois boules* [three balls] suspended in the air simultaneously!" From the depths of his cape, he brought forth a green cheesecloth bag and spun three mothballs into swift rotating motion.

Rentschler sprang up with a choked cry. "*Gobe-mouche* that I am! Blockhead!" he exclaimed. "Don't you see, Schneider? That's why the hollandaise laid those diners low—he used that very bag to squeeze the sauce, indifferent to the fact that it had contained mothballs! Seal the exits! Stop that man!" But it was too late; with a snarled imprecation, Moustique sprang toward the wings. In the shrill hubbub that ensued, I inexplicably found myself dancing a java with a comely grisette; then Rentschler,

25

flinging people aside like ninepins, was pulling me through a skylight and we were hurtling across the rooftops after our quarry. In reality, my associate explained as we hurtled, Moustique had left the Bobino in a cab, but protocol precluded our following him in any such mundane fashion.

"He's heading for the Ritz," panted the inspector. "A group of asparagus connoisseurs are holding their annual feed there tonight, which the columns of *Le Figaro* have been full of it for a week. Superfluous to add that if this blackguard, who is cooking for them under a nom de plume, compounds his lethal dressing, why the poor bastards will be stretched out in windows. I've a pretty—good—hunch, though," he panted on, clearing the Rue du Cherche-Midi with a bound, "that we're about to tie a kink in his mayonnaise whip."

WELL, we didn't. Two minutes afterward, Rentschler tripped over a loose gargoyle and dashed out his brains in the Quai Voltaire. I pressed on to the Ritz, but I must have crept in through the wrong dormer, because I wound up at a too, too marvellous gala at the Vicomtesse de Noailles'. Edith and Osbert and Sacheverell were there, and they gave me a simply divine recipe for my book. It's called Continental Upside-Down Chowchow, and here's what you do. You take a double handful of exotic locales . . .

The Hand That Cradles
the Rock

Pｃｒｄｏｎ ｍｅ, friends, but would you mind if I borrowed a corner of this lawn to faint dead away on? Go ahead with whatever you're doing; I just want to conk out until this roaring in my ears subsides. It's the damnedest sensation—somewhat as though I'd been pumped full of helium, tossed in a blanket, and shot through a wind tunnel. If I could only get these extremities to stop twitching . . . There, that's better. Christopher! Serves me right. I should have known what'd happen if I tangled, even remotely, with Fleur Fenton Cowles, today's editorial thunderhead and the most dynamic personality in the postwar publishing world. At least, that's the way someone named Mort Weisinger, billed as the editor of *Superman*, classifies her in the leading article of *The Writer's 1950 Year Book*, and if long intimacy with cloudborne genius means anything, the man certainly knows what he's talking about.

Mr. Weisinger's portrait of the versatile directress of *Look*, *Quick*, and *Flair*, whom no amount of keelhauling will persuade me to address by his emetic term of "boss-lady," depicts her as a high-voltage executive in whose personality a Kansas cyclone has been successfully wedded to Devonshire clotted cream. The vignette that introduces her and describes her accession to the throne of *Look* three years ago has a distinctly medieval tinkle:

"Behind a huge horseshoe-shaped desk in an office high above Fifth Avenue's sidewalks sat a straw-haired, sleekly groomed woman. Before her, on the luxurious carpet, stood three ranks of high-priced editorial and advertising brains. There was silence in the room while everyone waited for the slender, fragile woman to start talking. Deliberately, coolly, she let them wait, flipped the pages of a magazine dummy on her desk. When her right wrist moved, an eye-catching bracelet studded with pearls, rubies, and diamonds glittered in the sunlight. She spoke in a soft, gentle voice which almost cooed: 'It's been two weeks since I came to work on this magazine,' she began. 'You've all been sweet—too sweet—flattering me, buttering me up. I want you all to know that I've been in this game a long, long time. I've got a job to do here, and you're all going to help me. If not, heads will roll and fingers will be lopped off. That's all!'"

The whole scene is undeniably Florentine in feeling. The analogy is fortified a bit later when the author remarks, apropos of his subject's taste in jewels: "She is never without a huge one-inch Russian emerald ring. 'It's my trademark, it's me, it's Fleur—rough, uncut, vigorous,' *Time* magazine reports she said."

Enthralling as is the narrative of Fleur Cowles' meteoric climb to fame—copy writer, columnist, advertising-agency head, and vicereine of a publishing empire—it is Weisinger's account of her distinctive personal gifts that sets the thrushes singing in the reader's belly. "Fleur Cowles has a fantastic memory and her mnemonic powers would do credit to a Dunninger," reports her biographer. "Possibly because of her own uncanny memory, Fleur makes short shrift of hirelings whose retentive talents are not so prodigious. She is reputed to have fired a secretary who forgot to wind her office alarm clock, causing Fleur to miss an important engagement." A few lines later, Weisinger careers into another exceptional knack of Fleur's. "Fleur says she can breeze through a normal 120-page issue of *Time* in a half hour," he states, completely unaware that I myself hold the world's record of twenty-two seconds.

The roster of Fleur's accomplishments—her incessant travel, entertaining, and extracurricular activities—is an impressive one; I cull only two small blooms from Weisinger's nosegay as samples: "A former aviatrix with hundreds of hours in the air to her credit, Fleur has given up piloting, although she still holds a license. . . . Fleur paints a little, designs every stitch of her own clothes, designs her own jewelry, and even her glasses. 'I'm just a generally creative person,' she says modestly." The same stubborn honesty that prevents her from blinking her creative endowment emerges constantly at the office. "When she rejects a layout, a cover, or a project," says Weisinger, "she is apt to express her scorn with the fury of a hard-boiled city editor in a Hollywood front-page movie. 'Oh, I know I'm horribly blunt,' she admits. 'But if I think an idea is poor, I can't help coming right out and saying it's lousy. Yes, I'm direct.'" And again: "By the same token, she will fire an incompetent at the drop of a semicolon. 'I guess I'm just professionally intolerant of stupid people,' she confesses. 'I despise slow-witted persons, particularly in the creative fields. It's one of my biggest faults, but I can't help it.'" Could pitiless self-analysis go any further? Geez, it's like the "Confessions" of Jean-Jacques Rousseau.

The specific idiosyncrasy of Fleur's that crimps the heart into a waffle, however, is the exaggerated distrust Weisinger claims she displays toward her associates. "Because she is the wife of the Big Boss," he says, "Fleur Cowles has a fixation about being yessed-to-death by sycophantic staffers. To test their sincerity, she is always planning deliberate traps. At her conferences she will intentionally offer mediocre ideas of her own, invite criticisms. Employees who have the gumption to pooh-pooh these booby-traps win her confidence." If I interpret the foregoing rightly (and if I interpret it wrongly, I couldn't be more contrite), the pressure in a certain editorial sanctum must be roughly equivalent to that in the Mindanao Deep. I have been asking myself, between decreasing spells of vertigo, what life on such capricious levels is like. In the following morality, a webfooted attempt to approximate it, it should be borne in mind that the heroine is patterned after no actual boss-lady, living or dead. Like the immortal Topsy, she sprang full-blown from the forehead of Zeus. I'm just a generally creative person.

SCENE: *The office of Hyacinth Beddoes Laffoon, queen-pin of the pulp oligarchy embracing "Gory Story," "Sanguinary Love," "Popular Dissolution," and "Spicy Mortician." Hyacinth, poised and chic in a chiffon dress for which she herself spun the silk this morning, sits behind a gumshoe-shaped desk leafing through a copy of "Shroud," her latest fictional brain child. Standing alertly at attention before her, their Adam's apples moving up and down in unison, are Bunce, Van Lennep, Hagedorn, and Vishnu, her four editorial assistants.*

HYACINTH (*looking up abstractedly*): What's that chattering sound?

BUNCE (*eagerly*): It's Hagedorn's teeth, Mrs. Laffoon. I've been meaning to squeal on him the first opening I got. Gosh, you ought to hear the noise he makes over the partition! A man can hardly concentrate—

HYACINTH: Oh, you have trouble concentrating, do you?

BUNCE: No, no, no—it'd take a lot more than that to upset *me!* Why, I could work in a boiler factory!

HYACINTH: You may yet, the way you've been delivering around here. Meanwhile, Hagedorn, let's have those choppers out before the next conference. That is, if you last that long.

HAGEDORN (*quietly*): They'll be out right after lunch hour, Chief. You won't have to mention it again.

HYACINTH: Splendid. Now, then, I've had my ear to the ground recently and I get the impression some of you disagree with my policy on *Shroud.*

VAN LENNEP: Hell's bells, Hyacinth! Where'd you ever pick up that idea?

HYACINTH: From the dictaphone I had installed in the water cooler. (*Reading from a typed report*) "Just give the old windbag enough rope. You wait, the public'll pin back her ears." Does that sound familiar, Van Lennep?

VAN LENNEP: (*squirming*): I—I was talking about Miss Lovibond, who solicits those ads for bust developers and lost manhood. You said yourself we needed more tone.

HYACINTH: Well, all right, you twisted out of that one, but watch your step. I'm sentimental enough to think this organization can't function without one-hundred-per-cent loyalty.

VISHNU: And you've got it, Mrs. Laffoon. We worship the ground—

HYACINTH: At the same time, I won't stand for any soft soap or hogwash when I come up with a notion. The fact that Mr. Laffoon has ninety-three million dollars and owns all the real estate on Wacker Drive is beside the point. I want honest, sturdy, independent reactions—is that clear?

OMNES: Like crystal. . . . Gee, I wish I could express myself so forcefully! . . . Boy, what an editor! . . . etc.

HYACINTH: O.K. Well, I've just had a couple of hunches for brightening up *Shroud* that I'd like to try out on you. (*Quickly*) Oh, I know what you're going to say, that they *might* be feasible or that they *could* work—

HAGEDORN: No sirree, I can tell already they're world-beaters! A kind of a glow shines out of your face whenever you're on the beam.

HYACINTH: First, these covers we've been running. They're namby-pamby, no more punch than in a textbook. Look at this one—a naked girl tied to a bedpost and a chimpanzee brandishing a knout.

BUNCE: I see the structural weakness. It demands too much of the reader.

HYACINTH: Correct. We've got to drill him right between the eyes. Now, I visualize a cover with an aperture and a real revolver barrel protruding from it. With an acrid wisp of smoke curling out. Imagine that confronting you on a newsstand!

VISHNU: Where would the smoke be engendered?

HYACINTH: In a mechanism hinged to the back cover. To be sure, it's a trifle bulky and we might fall afoul of the smog ordinance in some areas—

VAN LENNEP (*ecstatically*): Nah, that can all be worked out! Baby, what a brain wave. It'll knock Publishers' Row right back on its heels!

HYACINTH: You think it's got undertow?

VAN LENNEP: Ho-ho, I can almost hear those dimes and nickels showering down!

HYACINTH: You bet you can; it's the cashier counting your severance pay. So long, Van Lennep, it's been nice knowing you. (*Sadly, as he leaves*) He just wouldn't learn. There's no room at Laffoon for a toady.

VISHNU: I knew it was a come-on from the start, Hyacinth. Did you notice how I gave a negative little shrug?

BUNCE: Me, too. I had difficulty in repressing a smile.

HAGEDORN: Smoke boxes on the back cover! Man, that was rich!

HYACINTH: Well, let's see how the next one appeals to you. You know, more and more of our younger readers are leaning toward marijuana, and I was wondering if we couldn't insert a complimentary sack in the body of the magazine, along with a trial book of cigarette papers. Might even approach Max Schling or some high-class florist to sponsor a special blend for us.

BUNCE: Mmm, that's a provocative slant. Trouble is it stirs me and yet it kind of leaves me cold. Thermally, it's ambivalent.

VISHNU: Ditto. I want to throw my arms around it but something indefinable holds me back.

HYACINTH: You, Hagedorn?

HAGEDORN: Straight from the shoulder, Mrs. Laffoon, it's as broad as it is long. How— How do you feel about it yourself?

HYACINTH: Well, naturally, it's my own idea—

VISHNU: Yes, and you can afford to crow. I know I'd be proud of it.

HYACINTH: I suspected you would. Personally, I think it's all wet.

VISHNU: (*thoughtfully*): Um. Maybe, if I hurry, I can ride down in the elevator with Van Lennep.

HYACINTH: Take your time—you've got oodles. (*He goes.*) There was just one other wrinkle that occurred to me, boys, but it's so idiotic I hesitate to mention it.

BUNCE: Aw, come on, Mrs. Laffoon. No matter how—er —amorphous it is, it might fire us—I mean it might lead to another angle.

HYACINTH: Well, it's this. Would there be any promotional value if we inserted several facsimile twenty-dollar bills into the binding, to serve as a blueprint for out-of-town readers who have to make their money at home?

BUNCE: I—ah—don't cotton to it, Hyacinth. We'd be accused of competing with *Popular Mechanics*.

HAGEDORN: It's basically a rural pitch. You'd expect to find it in *Capper's Weekly*.

HYACINTH: Yes, you're absolutely right. Thanks, men. It took plenty of guts to voice your frank, unvarnished opinion. (*They smirk.*) Still, if there was the teeniest chance it might benefit the magazine, we shouldn't block it with our pigheadedness, should we?

HAGEDORN (*paling*): We're not dead set against it— I say give it a whirl—

HYACINTH (*regretfully*): No. Deep down, there'd always be the lurking sense of guilt, the knowledge that we deliberately imperilled a valuable publishing property with our timidity. Sorry, gentlemen, it was my fault. I'll have to stay and face the music.

BUNCE: We could help you forget—

HYACINTH: It's white of you, but there are some bur-

35

dens a woman must carry alone. Goodbye. (*They exit. Velvet dusk veils the office, softening the lonely figure at the desk into a fragile, ghostly moth. Then, with a muted sigh, Hyacinth switches on her reading lamp, picks up a box of paper clips, and patiently begins constructing a linotype machine.*)

CURTAIN

CLOUDLAND REVISITED:

Why, Doctor, What Big Green Eyes You Have!

HALFWAY THROUGH the summer of 1916, I was living on the rim of Narragansett Bay, a fur-bearing adolescent with cheeks as yet unscarred by my first Durham Duplex razor, when I read a book that exerted a considerable influence on my bedtime habits. Up to then, I had slept in normal twelve-year-old fashion, with the lights full on, a blanket muffling my head from succubi and afreets, a chair wedged under the doorknob, and a complex network of strings festooned across the room in a way scientifically designed to entrap any trespasser, corporeal or not. On finishing the romance in question, however, I realized that the protection I had been relying on was woefully inadequate and that I had merely been crowding my luck. Every night thereafter, before retiring, I spent an extra half hour barricading the door with a chest of drawers, sprinkling tacks along the window sills, and strewing crumpled newspapers about the floor to warn me of approaching footsteps. As a minor added precaution, I slept under the bed, a ruse that did not make for refreshing slumber but at least threw my enemies off the scent. Whether it was constant vigilance or natural stamina, I somehow survived, and, indeed, received a surprising number of compliments on my appearance when I returned to grammar school that fall. I guess nobody in those parts had ever seen a boy with snow-white hair and a green skin.

Perhaps the hobgoblins who plagued me in that Rhode Island beach cottage were no more virulent than the reader's own childhood favorites, but the particular one I was introduced to in the book I've mentioned could hold up his head in any concourse of fiends. Even after thirty-five years, the lines that ushered him onstage still cause an involuntary shudder:

"Imagine, a person, tall, lean and feline, high-shouldered, with a brow like Shakespeare and a face like Satan, a close-shaven skull, and long, magnetic eyes of the true cat-green. Invest him with all the cruel cunning of an entire Eastern race, accumulated in one giant intellect, with all the resources of science, past and present, with all the resources, if you will, of a wealthy government— which, however, already has denied all knowledge of his existence. . . . This man, whether a fanatic or a duly appointed agent, is, unquestionably, the most malign and formidable personality existing in the world today. He is a linguist who speaks with almost equal facility in any of the civilized languages, and in most of the barbaric. He is an adept in all the arts and sciences which a great university could teach him. He also is an adept in certain obscure arts and sciences which *no* university of today can teach. He has the brains of any three men of genius. . . . Imagine that awful being, and you have a mental picture of Dr. Fu-Manchu, the yellow peril incarnate in one man."

Yes, it is the reptilian Doctor himself, one of the most sinister figures ever to slither out of a novelist's inkwell, and many a present-day comic book, if the truth were told, is indebted to his machinations, his underground laboratories, carnivorous orchids, rare Oriental poisons, dacoits, and stranglers. An authentic vampire in the great tradition, Fu-Manchu horrified the popular imagination in a long series of best-sellers by Sax Rohmer, passed through several profitable reincarnations in Hollywood, and (I thought) retired to the limbo of the second-hand bookshop, remembered only by a few slippered pantaloons like me. Some while ago, though, a casual reference by my daughter to Thuggee over her morning oatmeal made me prick up my ears. On close questioning, I found she had been bedevilling herself with "The Mystery of Dr. Fu-Manchu," the very volume that had induced my youthful fantods. I delivered a hypocritical little lecture, worthy of Pecksniff, in which I pointed out that Laurence Hope's "Indian Love" was far more suitable for her age level, and, confiscating the book, holed up for a retrospective look at it. I see now how phlegmatic I have become with advancing age. Apart from causing me to cry out occasionally in my sleep and populating my pillow with a swarm of nonexistent spiders, Rohmer's thriller was as abrasive to the nerves as a cup of Ovaltine.

THE PLOT OF "The Mystery of Dr. Fu-Manchu" is at once engagingly simple and monstrously confused. In essence, it is a duel of wits between the malevolent Celestial, who dreams of a world dominated by his countrymen, and Commissioner Nayland Smith, a purportedly brilliant sleuth, whose confidant, Dr. Petrie, serves as narrator. Fu-Manchu comes to England bent on the extermination of half a dozen distinguished Foreign Office servants, Orientalists, and other buttinskies privy to his scheme; Smith and Petrie constantly scud about in a web-footed attempt to warn the prey, who are usually defunct by the time they arrive, or busy themselves with being waylaid, sandbagged, drugged, kidnapped, poisoned, or garrotted by Fu-Manchu's deputies. These assaults, however, are never downright lethal, for regularly, at the eleventh hour, a beautiful slave of Fu-Manchu named Kâramanèh betrays her master and delivers the pair from jeopardy. The story, consequently, has somewhat the same porous texture as a Pearl White serial. An episode may end with Smith and Petrie plummeting through a trapdoor to nameless horrors below; the next opens on them comfortably sipping whiskey-and-soda in their chambers, analyzing their hairbreadth escape and speculating about the adversary's next move. To synopsize this kind of ectoplasmic yarn with any degree of fidelity would be to connive at criminal boredom, and I have no intention of doing so, but it might be fruitful to dip a spoon into the curry at random to gain some notion of its flavor.

Lest doubt prevail at the outset as to the utter malignancy of Fu-Manchu, the author catapults Nayland Smith into Petrie's rooms in the dead of night with the following portentous declaration of his purpose: "Petrie, I have travelled from Burma not in the interests of the British government merely, but in the interest of the entire white race, and I honestly believe—though I pray I may be wrong—that its survival depends largely on the success of my mission." Can Petrie, demands Smith, spare a few days from his medical duties for "the strangest business, I promise you, that ever was recorded in fact or fiction"? He gets the expected answer: "I agreed readily enough, for, unfortunately, my professional duties were not onerous." The alacrity with which doctors of that epoch deserted their practice has never ceased to impress me. Holmes had only to crook his finger and Watson went bowling away in a four-wheeler, leaving his patients to fend for themselves. If the foregoing is at all indicative, the mortality rate of London in the nineteen-hundreds must have been appalling; the average physician seems to have spent much less time in diagnosis than in mousing around Wapping Old Stairs with a dark lantern. The white race, apparently, was a lot tougher than one would suspect.

At any rate, the duo hasten forthwith to caution a worthy named Sir Crichton Davey that his life is in peril, and, predictably, discover him already cheesed off. His death, it develops, stemmed from a giant red centipede, lowered down the chimney of his study by Fu-Manchu's dacoits, regarding whom Smith makes the charmingly offhand statement "Oh, dacoity, though quiescent, is by no means extinct." Smith also seizes the opportunity to expatiate on the archcriminal in some fairly delicious double-talk: "As to his mission among men. Why did M. Jules Furneaux fall dead in a Paris opera-house? Because of heart failure? No! Because his last speech had shown that he held the key to the secret of Tongking. What became of the Grand Duke Stanislaus? Elopement? Suicide? Nothing of the kind. He alone was fully alive to Russia's growing peril. He alone knew the truth about Mongolia. Why was Sir Crichton Davey murdered? Because, had the work he was engaged upon ever seen the light, it would have shown him to be the only living Englishman who understood the importance of the Tibetan frontiers." In between these rhetorical flourishes, Petrie is accosted by Kâramanèh, Fu-Manchu's houri, who is bearing a deadly perfumed letter intended to destroy Smith. The device fails, but the encounter begets a romantic interest that saves Petrie's neck on his next excursion. Disguised as rough seafaring men, he and Smith have tracked down Fu-Manchu at Singapore Charlie's, an opium shop on the Thames dockside. Here, for the first time, Petrie gets a good hinge at the monster's eyes: ". . . their unique horror lay in a certain filminess (it made me think of the *membrana nictitans* in a bird) which, obscuring them as I threw wide the door, seemed to lift as I actually passed the threshold, revealing the eyes in all their brilliant viridescence." Before he can polish his ornithological metaphor, however, Petrie is plunged through a trapdoor into the river, the den goes up in flames, and it looks like curtains for the adventurous physician. But Providence, in the form of a hideous old Chinese, intervenes. Stripping off his ugly, grinning mask, he discloses himself as Kâramanèh; she extends her false pigtail to Petrie and, after pulling him to safety, melts into the night. It is at approximately this juncture that one begins to appreciate how lightly the laws of probability weighed on Sax Rohmer. Once you step with him into Never-Never Land, the grave's the limit, and no character is deemed extinct until you can use his skull as a paper-weight.

Impatient at the snail's pace with which his conspiracy is maturing, Fu-Manchu now takes the buttons off the foils. He tries to abduct a missionary who has flummoxed his plans in China, but succeeds only in slaying the latter's collie and destroying his manservant's memory—on the whole, a pretty footling morning's work. He then pumps chlorine gas into a sarcophagus belonging to Sir Lionel Barton, a bothersome explorer, with correspondingly disappointing results; this time the bag is another collie—sorry, a coolie—and a no-account ginzo secretary.

The villain's next foray is more heartening. He manages to overpower Smith and Petrie by some unspecified means (undoubtedly the "rather rare essential oil" that Smith says he has met with before, "though never in Europe") and chains them up in his noisome cellars. The scene wherein he twits his captives has a nice poetic lilt: "A marmoset landed on the shoulder of Dr. Fu-Manchu and peered grotesquely into the dreadful yellow face. The Doctor raised his bony hand and fondled the little creature, crooning to it. 'One of my pets, Mr. Smith,' he said, suddenly opening his eyes fully so that they blazed like green lamps. 'I have others, equally useful. My scorpions —have you met my scorpions? No? My pythons and hamadryads? Then there are my fungi and my tiny allies, the bacilli. I have a collection in my laboratory quite unique. Have you ever visited Molokai, the leper island, Doctor? No? But Mr. Nayland Smith will be familiar with the asylum at Rangoon! And we must not forget my black spiders, with their diamond eyes—my spiders, that sit in the dark and watch—then leap!' " Yet, having labored to create so auspicious a buildup, the author inexplicably cheats his suspense and lets it go for naught. No sooner has Fu-Manchu turned his back to attend to a poisoned soufflé in the oven than Kâramanèh pops up and strikes off the prisoners' gyves, and the whole grisly quadrille starts all over again. Smith and Petrie, without so much as a change of deerstalker hats, nip away to warn another prospective victim, and run full tilt into a covey of *phansigars*, the religious stranglers familiar to devotees of the *American Weekly* as Thugs. They outwit them, to be sure, but the pace is beginning to tell on Petrie, who observes ruefully, "In retrospect, that restless time offers a chaotic prospect, with few peaceful spots amid its turmoils." Frankly, I don't know what Petrie is beefing about. My compassion goes out, rather, to his patients, whom I envision by now as driven by default to extracting their own tonsils and quarrying each other's gallstones. *They're* the ones who need sympathy, Petrie, old boy.

With puff adders, tarantulas, and highbinders blooming in every hedge-row, the hole-and-corner pursuit of Fu-Manchu drums along through the next hundred pages at about the same tempo, resolutely shying away from climaxes like Hindus from meat. Even the episode in which Smith and Petrie, through the good offices of Kâramanèh, eventually hold the Doctor at gun point aboard his floating laboratory in the Thames proves just a pretext for further bombination about those filmy greenish eyes; a shower of adjectives explodes in the reader's face, and he is whisked off on a hunt for certain stolen plans of an aero-torpedo, an interlude that veers dangerously close to the exploits of the indomitable Tom Swift. The sequence that follows, as rich in voodoo as it is innocent of logic, is heavily fraught with hypnosis, Fu-Manchu having unaccountably imprisoned a peer named Lord Southery and Kâramanèh's brother Aziz in a cataleptic trance. They are finally revived by injections of a specific called the Golden Elixir—a few drops of which I myself could have used to advantage at this point—and the story sashays fuzzily into its penultimate phase. Accompanied by a sizable police detail, Smith, Petrie, and a Scotland Yard inspector surprise Fu-Manchu in an opium sleep at his hideout. A dénouement seems unavoidable, but if there was one branch of literary hopscotch Rohmer excelled in, it was avoiding dénouements. When the three leaders of the party recover consciousness (yes, the indispensable trapdoor again, now on a wholesale basis), they lie bound and gagged in a subterranean vault, watching their captor sacrifice their subordinates by pelting them with poisonous toadstools. The prose rises to an almost lyrical pitch: "Like powdered snow the white spores fell from the roof, frosting the writhing shapes of the already poisoned men. Before my horrified gaze, *the fungus grew;* it spread from the head to the feet of those it touched; it enveloped them as in glittering shrouds. 'They die like flies!' screamed Fu-Manchu, with a sudden febrile excitement; and I felt assured of something I had long suspected: that that magnificent, perverted brain was the brain of a homicidal maniac—though Smith would never accept the theory." Since no hint is given of what theory Smith preferred, we have to fall back on conjecture. More than likely, he smiled indulgently under his gag and dismissed the whole escapade as the prankishness of a spoiled, self-indulgent child.

The ensuing events, while gaudy, are altogether too labyrinthine to unravel. As a matter of fact they puzzled Rohmer, too. He says helplessly, "Any curiosity with which this narrative may leave the reader burdened is shared by the writer." After reading that, my curiosity shrank to the vanishing point; I certainly wasn't going to beat my brains out over a riddle the author himself did not pretend to understand. With a superhuman effort, I rallied just enough inquisitiveness to turn to the last page for some clue to Fu-Manchu's end. It takes place, as nearly as I could gather, in a blazing cottage outside London, and the note he addresses to his antagonists clears the way for plenty of sequels: "To Mr. Commissioner Nayland Smith and Dr. Petrie—Greeting! I am recalled home by One who may not be denied. In much that I came to do I have failed. Much that I have done I would undo; some little I have undone. Out of fire I came—the smoldering fire of a thing one day to be a consuming flame; in fire I go. Seek not my ashes. I am the lord of the fires! Farewell. Fu-Manchu."

I DARESAY it was the combination of this passage, the cheery hearth in front of which I reread it, and my under-wrought condition, but I thought I detected in the Doctor's valedictory an unmistakable mandate. Rising stealth-ily, I tiptoed up to my daughter's bedchamber and peered in. A shaft of moonlight picked out her ankles protruding from beneath the bed, where she lay peacefully sleeping, secure from dacoity and Thuggee. Obviously, it would take more than a little crackle of the flames below to arouse her. I slipped downstairs and, loosening the bind-ing of "The Mystery of Dr. Fu-Manchu" to insure a good supply of oxygen, consigned the lord of the fires to his native element. As he crumbled into ash, I could have sworn I smelled a rather rare essential oil and felt a pair of baleful green eyes fixed on me from the staircase. It was probably the cat, though I really didn't take the trou-

47

ble to check. I just strolled into the kitchen, made sure there was no trapdoor under the icebox, and curled up for the night. That's how phlegmatic a chap gets in later life.

Chewies the Goat but Flicks Need Hypo

It APPEARS TO BE more than a rumor that *Variety,* that reliable and colorful barometer of show business, may shortly change its name. According to my source (a papaya-juice vender on West Forty-sixth Street, whose identity I cannot disclose for fear of reprisals), the editors plan, by the simple expedient of altering three letters, to rechristen their paper *Anxiety,* a title more suited to its contents these days. This decision, between ourselves, comes as no surprise to me. Every Wednesday of late, skimming through *Variety's* picture grosses and film chatter, I have run into palpitations and anguish not normally aired outside the *American Journal of Orthopsychiatry.*

To judge from these bedside reports, the movie business is clearly *in extremis;* bats and mice are daily replacing audiences in theatres across the land, cobwebs are forming on the ushers, and exhibitors, hysterically accusing television, politics, substandard product, and even sunspots, have succumbed to panic. The most Talmudic reasons have been adduced to explain the decline in the box office, and it was inevitable that before long some Hawkshaw would try to pin the rap on that old whipping boy, the human stomach.

By the human stomach, of course, I refer in a broad, generic sense to the goodies—the caramel popcorn, molasses chews, coconut bars, and similar delicacies—sold in cinema lobbies. The suspicion has been gaining ground among showmen, says *Variety,* that "the annoyance of other customers' munch-crunch and the emphasis some houses are putting on selling of sweets" underlie the crisis. It quotes in support a conversation overheard by a member of the Allied Theatre Owners of Indiana. Four women sitting at the table next to him in a restaurant, he reported, "all agreed with one of the ladies, who said very emphatically that her family never attended the ———— theatre any more because they were tired of all the efforts made there to sell concessions, all the people in the audience munching during the show, and, most of all, having to sit through advertising trailers telling about how delicious were the concession-stand wares. Is it possible that theatre-lobby merchandising can be a factor why people are staying away from the movies, and is it worth a little restudy?"

Restudy, if I may make so bold, is not only indicated here; it is downright mandatory. The plain truth is that the Allied Theatre Owners of Indiana, and exhibitors generally, are staggering under a tremendous burden of mistaken, self-imposed guilt. As their patrons dwindle, keening about the pressures exerted on them to purchase sweets, the poor simps neurotically look inward for the reason instead of westward. The real culprit, I submit, is Hollywood itself. The industry has been locked too long in its ivory tower, too long preoccupied with artistic considerations better left to highbrows like Johnny Ruskin or Walt Pater. What the situation cries out for is pictures that will tell a gripping story and at the same time subtly sell the eatables in the lounge. With the aid of a small hand loom, I have woven a few necessary elements into an action-packed, down-to-earth yarn that may serve as a model, appealing to the gustatory as well as the visual instinct. It may not wheedle customers into the show shop, but at least it will act as a tourniquet.

WE FADE IN on the porte-cochère of a mansion ablaze with lights, and, as sleek motors laden with impeccably groomed men of aristocratic visage and women garbed in the *dernier cri* from Paris disgorge their human freight, establish that this is the home of Monica, Lady Beltravers, arbiter of Bombay society. Monica, an Irene Dunne-type chatelaine that is the very essence of the chicly poised

British gentlewoman, loiters on the stoop greeting her
guests. "Sir Cyprian Chetwynd—what a surprise!" she
exclaims cordially to one imperious, hawk-nosed oldster
as he alights from his equipage. "I certainly never expected the Home Secretary himself at my ball, crowning
event of the social season albeit it is!" To another arrival,
a swarthy potentate in whose turban glows a single magnificent ruby, she observes laughingly, "Well, Hara Singh,
I guess we will not be having to press our crystal chande-
lier into service, now that the Star of Assam is shedding
its beam on the courtly throng!" From hints like the foregoing, it is blueprinted that her Ladyship's annual rout is
the smartest affair in the Punjab, and that even the Vice-
roy would count himself lucky to get the nod from her.
Monica, the cynosure of all eyes, wears on her queenly
head the famous Beltravers tiara, and as we truck indoors
with her through the assemblage, we garner numerous
startled reactions. (The reactions are startled not because
she is wearing the tiara on her head, where it should be,
but because of its splendor.) Everybody thinks she is
goofy to display so costly a bauble, for is it not an open
secret that Tony Pickering, the most elusive international-
society jewel thief in the Empire, is somewhere in the
area, pledged to steal it from under the fair owner's nose?
Monica, notwithstanding, snaps her pretty fingers at the
ravens who croak disaster, graciously urging them to sample the lavish feed arrayed on the sideboard—turkey,
tongue in aspic, slaw, and suchlike viands. And right here,
without slackening pace, is an ideal spot to slip in an off-

beat allusion to the comestibles available to moviegoers in the lobby.

"Bless me, Monica, what a toothsome collation," remarks one of the dowagers, enviously scanning it through her lorgnette.

"Thanks, Baroness," Lady Beltravers replies. "And, speaking of matters edible, the fans watching this need not fall prey to the green-eyed monster, for adjacent to their chairs they will lamp a pleasing selection of mint drops, chocolate creams, and candied apples to beguile themselves stomach-wise." Needless to say, I am not writing dialogue, just spitballing to indicate how smoothly the pitch blends in with the action.

To pick up our story thread: Unsuspected by the merrymakers, Tony Pickering, a debonair figure in flawless tails (Randolph Scott), saunters nonchalantly amid the waltzing couples. The Beltravers tiara is almost within his grasp. Suddenly, he comes face to face with Sandra Thrale (Greer Garson), the second-most-elusive society jewel thief in the Empire. A sardonic situation, fraught with boffs—two devil-may-care tricksters bent on the same perilous mission. Who will emerge victor? The lovers (for so they soon prove to be, despite their mutual antagonism) strike a bargain, snatch the prize in some ingenious fashion as yet to be devised, and show their pursuers a clean pair of heels. Sprinkled through the chase I see a couple of knockabout Hindu comics, on the order of Karl Dane and George K. Arthur, whose uproarious antics constantly land them in hot water and reap a rich harvest of laffs.

This concludes the first sequence, a high-octane mixture of suspense, comedy, and romance guaranteed to keep people on the edge of their seats but still not allow them full mobility.

SIDI-BEL-ABBÈS, headquarters of the French Foreign Legion. Sand ... heat ... primitive passions fanned into flame by a word, a look. Into this port of nameless men drifts the flotsam of many races, asking only one thing—to forget. And with it, seeking salvation under the remorseless African sun, has come Tony Pickering. He and Sandra, after a senseless quarrel in Rome, during which she cast the tiara into the Tiber in a fit of pique, have broken. We iris down on him idling through the bazaars shortly before his regiment leaves for El Kébir, a remote desert outpost. A vivid background and a perfect opportunity to insinuate a timely message to the savages out front.

"Look, *mon capitaine*," a merchant whines, plucking at Tony's sleeve. "Splendid fresh figs, succulent as a Bedouin maid."

"Yes, and just as tricky," comments Pickering acidly. "That's where folks buying peanuts in their neighborhood flicks have the jump on us creatures of the silver screen. Those tasty goobers, warranted bacteria-free, speed directly from the roaster into sanitized glassine bags and thence to grateful palates. Boy, I could eat a slew of them." In other words, rather than hit the patrons over

54

the head with a crass commercial, we actually use it to further the narrative. From now on, every man, woman, and child in the building is psychologically primed to rush out and give his taste buds a treat, except that the action is moving so fast he dassn't tear himself away.

We now deliver a surprise twist, a terrific sock that nobody but a clairvoyant could anticipate. In the ordinary scenario, the next scene would portray El Kébir beleaguered by tribesmen; Tony and brutal Sergeant Lepic (Brod Crawford), the only survivors in the fort, have posted their dead comrades on the parapet with rifles in their hands to hoodwink the attackers when a relief column led by Sandra (who has followed her swain unbeknownst to Algeria) raises the siege. Instead of this tepid dénouement, which would merely generate yawns, we dissolve to a hunting lodge in the Canadian Rockies, where Sandra's wealthy father (Charles Coburn) has taken her to cure her infatuation for Tony. Since their spat in Rome, the girl has paid her debt to society and become a brilliant woman psychiatrist, a leader in her profession. Yet—irony of ironies—she, who brings happiness to others, is denied it herself, for Cupid has laid waste her heart. She cannot decide between Tony, now a world-famed construction engineer, and Jim Stafford (John Wayne), New York's most outstanding criminal lawyer. As father and daughter breakfast in their mountain retreat, unaware that a consuming forest fire rages toward them, the kindly old millionaire is concerned anent her birdlike appetite.

"You haven't eaten a crumb, sweet," Thrale chides her.

"Try one of these speckled beauties which I captured it with rod and reel outside our door this morning."

"They *are* scrumptious, Daddy," she makes wistful reply, "but you'll never know bliss till you tackle Frosticles, the jet-powered ice-cream sensation." Thrale's curiosity is piqued, as anyone's would be, and he inquires where the confection may be obtained, whereupon Sandra enlightens him. The scene can be made doubly effective by dispatching candy-butchers down the aisle on cue, shouting "Frosticles!" They should, however, be cautioned against shouting so loud that the audience loses the thread. Once that happens, the jig is up.

THE FRAMEWORK of the story being elastic, we now have two possibilities to milk for a climax. In one, Tony and Jim, who have renounced their careers to be near Sandra and are loggers in a lumber camp close by, fight a sensational watery duel for her hand with peaveys. The flames soon bring them to their senses and, good-naturedly laying aside their rivalry, they race to save the trapped pair, but they arrive too late. Since this line is a little on the defeatist side, it might be better to develop the other, a device that gives the plot a neat switch. We lap-dissolve to a primitive raft becalmed in the South Pacific and plant that Tony, Jim, and four Norwegian buddies have all but given up hope for the success of their expedition. Tony has staked his reputation as a world-famous anthologist to prove that certain old-time Peruvians migrated to Tahiti on a raft made of balsam logs. The gallant sextet's provisions have run short, and in his delirium each man dreams longingly of his favorite dish on terra firma. If only he could feel the icy trickle of a cola drink between his parched lips, muses Tony, or nibble the delectable taffy that even the humblest filmgoer has at his beck and call. The various dainties pass in review in balloons over his head, to hammer the point home to the most obtuse. And then we belt into a sizzling washup. A typhoon strikes the frail craft, the seafarers are drenched to the bone, and one of the Norwegians is revealed to be Sandra, who has renounced her psychiatric career to be near Tony. As they joyfully nestle in each other's arms, the cry of "Polynesia ho!" echoes from the yardarm. Tony's scientific thesis is vindicated, Jim sportingly acknowledges him the better man, and we squeeze on a tag wherein the couple sails homeward to the strains of "Aloha Oe." By then, the projectionist can breeze right into "Coming Attractions," for the patrons will be streaking toward the lobby to gorge themselves or apply for refunds, as the case may be.

Well, there it is—no "Intolerance" or "Gone with the Wind," I grant you, but a nice, sound program film that'll hold up its end on any double bill and yield a good many mandolin picks after the run is finished. I've even written a score for it, containing half a dozen songs of "Hit Parade" calibre, and if Hammerstein's fee is excessive, I'll throw in a hatful of lyrics for good measure. The main thing is to release it pronto and get rid of all that glucose in the lobby before the mice get at it. You don't want sagebrush growing in your bathtub, do you, Mr. Selznick?

Salesman,
Spare that Psyche

LET'S HAVE a show of hands—how many people here know what they'd like to be in their next incarnation? I mean if you had your choice, would you want to be, say, the curator of the British Museum or a crackerjack circus aerialist or the best of breed at the Empire Cat Show or what? Every thoughtful person interested in which way his soul is going to jump, whether he subscribes to the Buddhist system of musical chairs or not, must have asked himself this question at one time or another, and inasmuch as I happen to have just stumbled on an ideal future identity, with about as much omnipotence as anyone could ever hope to attain, I'd like to register it before it's snapped up. Comes the transmigration, I want to be vice-president in charge of sales of a twenty-million-dollar cosmetics corporation. Not any old vice-president but one in particular—a chap named Martin Revson. Martin Revson can be me if he likes, or if he wishes to sublet to some other tenant, we can work that out, too. He'll find me perfectly flexible.

My admiration for Mr. Revson, I hasten to say, is in no way vitiated by the fact that up till yesterday I didn't know him from Adam's off ox. It was an interview in a recent issue of *Business Week*, entitled "Smart Words, Quality, and Freud," that introduced me to the man and, specifically, to his technique for salvaging sterile personnel, possibly the most singular in American industry. Using a portable microphone to capture the full, idiomatic flavor of Revson's words, *Business Week* cornered the executive to ascertain how the Revlon Products Corporation launches and sells new makeup aids. The beautycoon, as I flinch at calling him, opened his heart. "The reason women buy cosmetics," he said, laying his nose slyly alongside his finger, "is because they buy hope. In other words," he added, glomming a phrase from an impractical *schlemiel* named Henry David Thoreau, who gets himself quoted in the damnedest contexts, "most women lead lives of dullness, quiet desperation, and I think cosmetics are a wonderful escape from it." He then cited a liquid foundation called Touch and Glow that apparently confers powers of escape analogous to those enjoyed by Harry Houdini, and recounted how this product was born, packaged, publicized, and merchandised. By and large, his revelations were a shade less than epochal, but one minor disclosure about the mechanics of radio publicity deserves mention: "Well, those things are done sort of inadvertently —what you do is go to see Hope or Skelton or somebody of that nature and tell them about your new product coming out with, oh, a couple of million dollars in advertising, and then the script writer writes it in. We try to plan it with the writer and say—here, this script you are using two weeks hence, if you have a chance to use it—if you've got a girl in there that is known to be funny on the program for eight or ten weeks, and he says she has the Touch and Glow look, that would bring an ordinary yak from the people listening in. So that's the way we get it in—sort of inadvertently." The easy negligence of the whole thing is truly captivating. For sheer insouciance, nothing could surpass the spectacle of an incipient Mark Twain grinding out cosmetic yaks with a two-million-dollar pitchfork lightly pinking his bottom. No wonder the corridors of Radio City are gritty with Benzedrine.

The crux of the interview, however, was Revson's exposition of his company's policy toward its unproductive salesmen. "Incidentally, what about these sales meetings I hear about called Psycho-Revlons?" his inquisitor demanded. "What exactly are they? Why are they called 'psycho'?" Pared down to essentials, the answers run as follows: "Well, we feel that the salesman may not be as good as he appears to be outwardly. And he has to be analyzed when his sales are not good. He doesn't recognize, unless he is analyzed, what the hell is the matter with him. Now, instead of firing men, we have salvaged them—men with brains and intelligence—merely by using the Psycho-Revlon method. Sitting a man down and reviewing with him all the things that are wrong with him. Even though the man may be in his forties . . . Further than that, we show scenes—action scenes and motion pictures of live actors—depicting the mental blocks that arise in a salesman's mind, and we try to remove those mental blocks."

PERHAPS we can best evaluate Revlon's sales clinic by visiting a similar rehabilitation center at the Sassoon Tweezer Corporation, world's largest manufacturers of styptic pencils. It is one of the contradictions of our highly complex society that the Sassoon Tweezer Corporation should market nothing but styptic pencils, whereas the Sassoon Pencil Corporation controls the entire tweezer output. Ah, well, far better leave such anomalies to wiser heads and raise the curtain.

SCENE: *A Psycho-Sassoon, about eleven o'clock in the morning. The setting is a small, trapezoid-shaped chamber draped with yards of filmy gray cheesecloth, calculated to convey an atmosphere of intense cerebration. Since this décor, in addition to being hideously inflammable, tends to engulf the dramatis personae, they may have to spend most of the action in a crouching position, with fire extinguishers playing over them, but a good actor can project anywhere. Three men are discovered on-stage:*

Salesman, Spare that Psyche

Loudermilk, vice-president in charge of sales; Bultitude, a district supervisor; and Folger, a salesman.

BULTITUDE (*angrily*): What's the use of coddling the little skunk, Mr. Loudermilk? I say kick him out on his tail and be done with it.

LOUDERMILK: Tut, tut, no point in bullying the fellow. We'll never straighten him out if you take that line.

BULTITUDE: Well, I give up. I wash my hands. *You* deal with him. (*He flings away in a pet, promptly entangles himself in the draperies, and spends the rest of the production struggling to work free.*)

LOUDERMILK (*frowning over a report*): This sales chart of yours, Folger—it's a mite baffling.

FOLGER: In what way, sir?

LOUDERMILK: Well, according to your breakdown, you've just made a three-week swing through the Middle Atlantic States and sold over six million dollars' worth of styptic pencils.

FOLGER: You said it. I guess that's pretty near an all-time record.

LOUDERMILK: It is. The only trouble is we've checked with ten or fifteen of the retailers and they disclaimed ever ordering the goods.

FOLGER: No kidding.

LOUDERMILK: Furthermore, none of them remembered ever seeing you. Didn't know your name, in fact.

FOLGER: I couldn't have made a very deep impression, could I?

LOUDERMILK: No, not if you didn't go into the stores.

FOLGER: You've got a point there, Mr. Loudermilk.

LOUDERMILK: Man to man, Folger—have you ever been in the Middle Atlantic States?

FOLGER: To the best of my recollection, no, sir.

LOUDERMILK: Under the circumstances, then, these orders can hardly be construed as binding, can they?

FOLGER: Well-l-l, if you want to be technical . . .

LOUDERMILK: What do you suggest we do now?

FOLGER: Of course, I can always resign—if you feel you can dispense with a man who brings in six million dollars' worth of business.

LOUDERMILK: I think you incline to be a faulty logician at times. I mean to say those orders are more or less mythical, aren't they?

FOLGER: That's so. I keep forgetting.

LOUDERMILK: Your expense account, on the other hand, is, regrettably, all too real. Do you recall any details of that?

FOLGER: Er—no. Would you mind refreshing me?

LOUDERMILK: Not in the least. It comes to about forty-five hundred, including the champagne.

FOLGER: Well, I certainly loved every moment of it. And I'm confident Gloria would agree. (*As Loudermilk's eyebrows elevate*) My sweetie. *Petite amie,* as the French say.

LOUDERMILK: Oh? I—er—I had always understood you were a respectable married man.

FOLGER: I'd like to see anyone better qualified. I've got wives in three different cities.

LOUDERMILK: Look here, Folger, I'm going to talk to

you straight from the shoulder. A man's private life is his own—

FOLGER: Check. Everybody's entitled to a little fun on the side.

LOUDERMILK: Sure he is. For instance, I have a babe tucked away in a nest on Seventy-third Street, and I tell you she's been an inspiration to me. By the way, you won't say anything to Mrs. Loudermilk about this?

FOLGER: Not unless I need a quick century note or the equivalent. You know how it is when you get caught in a squeeze.

LOUDERMILK: You bet I do. Just come around any time and I'll help you out. No, what I'm driving at is your work.

FOLGER (*peevishly*): Oh, shoot, do we have to go into that now? I promised to meet Gloria at Jaeckel's and look at a broadtail coat.

LOUDERMILK: This shouldn't take more than a few minutes. You see, I have a hunch your whole sales approach is wrong. There's some sort of mental block or kink that prevents you from functioning properly, and I'm going to iron it out. Press that switch on the desk, will you? (*As Folger complies, the room darkens and a screen lights up at rear.*)

FOLGER (*enchanted*): Oh, boy! Movies!

LOUDERMILK: You like them, eh?

FOLGER: I eat 'em up. I go to two, three every afternoon.

LOUDERMILK: Well, this one's kind of special, because you appear in it. (*Folger starts.*) Now, don't get panicky; it's all in the family and I'm only showing it to help you.

The Ill-Tempered Clavichord

We made it with a concealed camera in a Syracuse drug-store. Remember that trip?

FOLGER: Not very well, sir. I was plastered a good deal of the time.

LOUDERMILK: It'll come back to you. (*A white-coated figure, backed by shelves of pharmaceuticals, settles into focus.*) There, that's the prospect—old man Hornaday, isn't it?

FOLGER: In person, and, brother, what a crab.

LOUDERMILK: No, just a misfit. Doesn't know how to get along with salesmen. O.K., here's a shot from the reverse angle as you come in.

FOLGER: Oops, look at that display of yoghurt. I really knocked that for a loop.

LOUDERMILK: Hornaday should have fastened it down, he'll have a lawsuit one of these days. This next part's a trifle blurred. You seem to be tangling with a customer.

FOLGER: Ah, some wacky dame. She tried to inveigle me into the phone booth.

LOUDERMILK: Oh, that's why she's slapping you; I couldn't figure out. Anyway, here you've finished wiping off the lipstick and you start your pitch to Hornaday.

FOLGER: Wait a minute. Something's been omitted. What's he grappling me by the seat of the pants for?

LOUDERMILK: We're really lost without a sound track. If you could reconstruct your dialogue, maybe we could analyze your failure to clinch the sale.

FOLGER: Search me. I gave him the standard buildup. "Ever nick yourself shaving?" I said. When he said yes, I sprang the convincer I've been using. "Try an electric razor," I said, "and you can laugh at styptic pencils." I can't imagine why—Holy mackerel!

LOUDERMILK (*encouragingly*): Go ahead, lad. I think I know what you're going to say.

FOLGER: It just dawned on me. I was touting him off styptic pencils without realizing it!

LOUDERMILK: Exactly. Instead of *selling* the product, you were *undermining* it. What we call the will to stop eating.

FOLGER: (*snuffling*): Oh, my God, how could anybody be so blind?

LOUDERMILK: Don't reproach yourself, old man. In the dark, subterranean river of the unconscious we all have these lurks quirking.

FOLGER: Quirks lurking, you mean. Take the mush out of your mouth.

LOUDERMILK (*apologetically*): I'm sorry. After you get into your forties, you—well, you slip a cog now and then. Like poor Bultitude, there, for instance—look at him floundering around in that cheesecloth.

FOLGER: Poor Bulitude nothing. There's no room in a high-pressure business organization for weaklings. If you can't fish, cut bait. If you can't cut bait, get out.

LOUDERMILK: Folger, you're dead right. Listen, we need a district supervisor with energy and imagination. Anybody who can think in terms of six-million-dollar orders is good enough for me. How soon can you step into Bultitude's shoes?

FOLGER: Well, I'd sort of like to talk it over with my wives.

The Ill-Tempered Clavichord

LOUDERMILK: Do that, and, what's more, take a couple of weeks in White Sulphur Springs at our expense. We want you back on the job in fighting trim.

FOLGER: Thanks, Chief, I feel like a new man. Who knows? One of these days you might even have a vacancy here for a vice-president in charge of sales.

LOUDERMILK (*tolerantly*): Now, now, boy, you've just found your pin-feathers. You haven't yet begun to fly.

FOLGER: No, but to punch home your avian simile, I'll never lack for worms as long as you hold onto that little nest in Seventy-third Street. So long, Doc, and love to Mrs. Loudermilk. (*He exits whistling. His superior stares after him, plunged in a brown study. Then, reaching for the telephone directory, he begins scrabbling through it for the number of "Business Week."*)

CURTAIN

CLOUDLAND REVISITED:
Antic Hey-Hey

PERHAPS the saltiest observation Max Beerbohm made in "Seven Men," a book whose saline content has remained as high and delightful as it was on its appearance thirty years ago, occurs in that matchless story of a literary vendetta, "Hilary Maltby and Stephen Braxton." Writing about the preoccupation of contemporary novelists with sprites and woodland gods—Maltby, it will be recalled, was the author of "Ariel in Mayfair" and Braxton of "A Faun in the Cotswolds"—Beerbohm remarked, "From the time of Nathaniel Hawthorne to the outbreak of the war, current literature did not suffer from any lack of fauns." I suppose this reflection has always struck me as especially astute because when I originally encountered it, back in 1923, I happened to be in a milieu where satyrs and dryads, Silenus and Bacchic revels, were as common as cattails in a Jersey swamp. Its impact was heightened, moreover, by the fact that I was just convalescing (although for a while my reason was despaired of) from the effects of a tumultuous, beauty-bound best-seller of the period called "Wife of the Centaur," by Cyril Hume.

The place was Brown University, and the particular focus of all this mythological activity was a literary magazine by the name of *Casements,* on whose staff I had a brief, precarious toehold as assistant art editor. At least three-quarters of the text of *Casements* each month was made up of villanelles, rondels, pantoums, and ballades in which Pan pursued laughing nymphs through leafy bowers, and it was my job to provide decorative headings and tailpieces to complement them. Fortunately, I had a steady hand and an adequate supply of tracing paper, and if my superiors had not accidentally stumbled on the two albums of Aubrey Beardsley I was cribbing my drawings from, I might have earned an enviable reputation.

My short and brilliant tenure had one positive result, however; I finally discovered what was inspiring the Arcadian jingles I illustrated. One afternoon, while dawdling around the dormitory room of our chief troubadour and waiting for him to shellac a madrigal about cloven hoofs in the boscage, I picked up a novel bound in orange and gold and read a passage he had underscored. "Ho!" it ran. "The centaur is born! Child's body and colt's body, birth-wet and asprawl in the ferns. What mother will nourish

this wild thing? Who will foster this beast-god? Where
will he grow? In what strange cavern will he make his
bed, dreaming his amazing dreams? What shaggy tutor
will teach him as he lolls with his head on nature's breast?
What mortal maid will he carry away to his upland pas-
tures in terror and delight?"

"Hot puppies!" I burst out excitedly. "This isn't prose—
it's frozen music! The gink who wrote this is the bee's
knees!"

"Yes, yes," said the poet guiltily, plucking the book out
of my hands. "I—er—I haven't read it myself, but I guess
it's had a wide influence." It was a Freudian slip on his
part, which some instinct told me was worth investigating,
and when I did, my suspicions were confirmed. Not only
he but practically every bard on *Casements* had been
using "Wife of the Centaur" as a water hole. The oppor-
tunities for blackmail were, of course, illimitable, and
had my own nose been clean (the Beardsley complication
was just breaking), I might have taken advantage of them.
The truth is, though, that on reading the book I succumbed to its witchery so completely that I, too, began
writing villanelles and pantoums in the same idiom. Sad
to say, they never saw printer's ink; my colleagues, jealous
of the applause the verses might excite, stopped publishing
Casements altogether, and overnight a potential Words-
worth again became a drab little sophomore.

A WEEK or so ago, standing with nostrils atwitch and a
pocketful of rusty change over the bargain table of a Fifty-

ninth Street bookstore, I spotted a copy of Mr. Hume's chef-d'oeuvre and, unable to resist a cut-rate sentimental pilgrimage into the past, gave it a home. Its effect, after a lapse of twenty-seven years, was not quite as dynamic as I had anticipated. Rather than quickening me to an orgy of spondees and dactyls, it slowed down my heartbeat to that of a turtle's and enveloped me in a profound slumber under a grape arbor, where I narrowly escaped being consumed by a colony of ants. It may sound unfair to suggest that they were attracted by the rich and sticky imagery of the book, but from now on I plan to restrict my open-air reading to the *World Almanac,* with a Flit gun cocked across my knee to repel browsers.

Since "Wife of the Centaur" is the tale of a sensitive boy who grows up to be a poet, it quite properly begins with a salvo of rapturous and yeasty verse to help you adjust your emotional sights. The following, one of several quatrains introducing a fifty-page pastiche of Jeffrey Dwyer's childhood, gives a hasty but reliable preview of the feature picture:

> The centaurs awoke! they aroused from their beds of pine,
> Their long flanks hoary with dew, and their eyes deep-drowned
> In the primal slumber of stones, stirred bright to the shine!
> And they stamped with their hooves, and their gallop abased the ground!

Jeffrey, it is shortly established, is an infant centaur, in what might be described as cushy circumstances; he attends an exclusive private school in Connecticut, preparing for Yale, and, when not saturating himself in "The

Oxford Book of English Verse," struggles tormentedly under the lash of awakening sex. The description of the process discloses him to be a pretty full-blooded lad: "Lean desire wrapped his body in taut coils, oppressing him like pain. . . . Lust was a blind force, immeasurable, overwhelming, irresistible as a toppling wall of black water. . . . And desire, the gaunt beast, buffeted and shook him. . . . 'God! God!' . . . The air was a voice that hissed hot promises of forbidden mysteries, the trees were erotic minstrels singing old songs of shameful loves." Luckily for Jeffrey, if not for the reader, his adolescent libido is channelled into writing verse before it lays waste to the Nutmeg State, and while the samples furnished are hardly calculated to set the Housatonic on fire—packed as they are with fantasies of whitely radiant madonnas with golden coils of hair and cherry-red lips moving in strange benedictions—it is clear that Calliope has destined the youngster for the business end of a quill.

The heroine of the book, a conventional maiden named Joan Converse, in the same affluent social stratum, now makes her advent with a clash of cymbals and another fifty pages of adolescent background. Joan's sexual yearnings do not seem quite as turbulent as Jeffrey's, but she gets a symbolical sendoff just as rousing: "Ohé hamadryad, lurking in yon covert of ruddy sumac, are your cheeks red with remembered dreaming? Hark! Hark, little maid with the limbs of a slim cascade—hark, for the young centaur tramples and neighs along the wooded hillside, no longer far away. And you do not flee, little maid with your rose-petal cheeks? Ah, the centaur! Ho, hamadryad!" It is futile to begin slavering and speculating on the explosion the two will eventually create, though, because their paths do not converge for years, and by the time they do, at a Long Island house-party, the third leg of the triangle is already in place. Jeffrey, during the interval, has been distinguishing himself at Yale as a poet and tosspot, and is currently dangling after Inez Martin, a heartless flirt whose eyes range from clear gray to transparent green with her varying moods. "She's a willow beside a brook of running water, and the sun on both," the poet epitomizes her to Joan, brokenly recounting the indignities Inez has subjected him to. Irksome as the maternal role is, Joan sensibly bides her time and is rewarded in the Easter vacation, when Jeffrey buckles under her own glamour in the rear seat of a Stutz. He kisses her roughly, impetuously; as she goes faint at the contact of his slim, strong hands, she notices that "they seemed to have an eager, fine life of their own. Tense and flexible and swift as blood horses." Much to Joan's chagrin, alas, it is merely a routine workout for the ponies. Reining them in before they can bolt, Jeffrey warns her that something horrible might have happened, that she must never let anyone again kiss her in such abandoned fashion. "'Me least of all,' he said harshly. Then he bent down and kissed the cool palm of her hand." And so, in a bittersweet dying fall that combines echoes of Havre de Grace, Jergen's Lotion, and the code of a Yale gentleman, is born the romance of Joan Converse, occupation hamadryad, and Jeffrey Dwyer, jongleur and centaur.

Actually, despite all the preliminary huffing and puffing,

nothing concrete develops between them in the ensuing third of the story, for Jeffrey still has to fight the First World War and purge Inez from his system. He cleans up the first, and obviously easier, assignment in a brisk ten pages, throws himself into a journalistic career, and makes a superhuman but fruitless pitch for Joan's rival. How greatly she disturbs him may be gauged from this saucy vignette: "Her blouse was deeply opened at the neck, showing a long V of glowing flesh with a faint shadow at the point. One foot was drawn up under her and Jeffrey caught a glimpse of a rosy knee with the stocking rolled below it. . . . Happiness pierced him suddenly like a flaming sword. His pulses beat to the rhythm of a wild prothalamion. . . . He! For him! He was to explore the shrouded mysteries that dwelt behind her eyes. Her Venus body and the youth of it, the promises he read in the sultry curves of her mouth . . . these were his to take and hold like a cup, to drink deep. . . ." The goodies, maddeningly, remain just out of reach; Inez has pledged herself to a wastrel named Jack Todd, and, sick with disillusion, Jeffrey plunges into a stormy cycle of wenching and boozing that climaxes in the arms of a lady of the town. Slowly and painfully, his equilibrium returns, a salvage operation that calls forth fresh flights of lyricism: "Now is the centaur weary of men and men's ways. . . . Centaur, is your beast's spirit broken? Is your man's heart crushed utterly? No! For now the centaur shouts anew his loud defiance! . . . I will go back again to taste the bright hill-water of my colthood and my nostrils shall know as of old the thin air of my mountain realms. I shall lie upon a bed of ferns

75

under familiar constellations. . . . In the still of the night, in an hour when quiet comes upon the crickets and all the little creatures of the dark, I shall reach up with my hand and pluck that round honeycomb, the moon, out of the sky to feed my hunger."

Reduced to prosaic, taxpayer's lingo, this means that Jeffrey goes back to his prep school, engages in a purifying bull session with the headmaster, sobers up, finishes a novel called "Squads Right About" debunking war, and publishes it to wide critical acclaim. Joan, who meanwhile has lain obligingly dormant for a hundred pages waiting for her swain to unsnarl his glands, hereupon pops back into view. Just why she and Jeffrey should plight their troth at the Museum of Natural History, I was unable to fathom, except that it affords the hero an opportunity to indulge in some verbal pyrotechnics on science—or, rather, his conception of it. "Geology, Joan!" he exclaims. "God, but I love geology! Astronomy! The gorgeous tremendousness of it! Science for gods! . . . Your mind goes tramping through space like a hobo in spring, with spiral nebulas trailing at its ankles like gobs of cobwebs. You want to howl and kick suns around because then you realize that the human mind is the greatest created thing." At any rate, after a plethora of similar brainy generalizations, Jeffrey providentially runs out of saliva, and the two dissolve into an embrace that leads to the altar and the next movement of the symphony, a section stylishly entitled "Lilith's Garden."

"Lilith's Garden" is ecstasy unconfined by whalebone, chaperone, or censor, a honeymoon that makes most

other fictional ones I can recall seem vapid by comparison. The newlyweds spend it at a seaside cottage on
Long Island, whooping around the dunes and behaving
in a thoroughly heathen and unfettered fashion: "At night
on the beach, he would suddenly make a horrible face and
howl, 'I'm a remora!' or 'I'm a mandrake!' or even 'I'm a
Calvinist!' Then he would growl and come after her in
great fantastic leaps, flinging out his arms and legs and
she would squeal and try to double back to the deserted
steamer rug." The proximity of salt water, naturally,
brings on a whole new rush of metaphor, and the hamadryad switches into a mermaid: "And when he kissed her
mouth he tasted the brine of the deep places where her
home was; and her dripping arms crept around his
neck to draw him under and carry him down forever
to a palace of pale coral where fish darted like birds in a
garden." As if these quincelike frivolities were already
not sufficient to pucker up one's lips, they are punctuated
by scolding comments from an old Irish retainer of Joan's
playfully known as Madsy, a dialectician of the school of
Harrigan and Hart: "Didn't I hear the both of yez on the
beach last night carryin' on like wild pagan creatures?
Half the night you was up behavin' scandleous and undai-
cent as though there wasn't that much of a Christian soul
between yez! . . . When you might better have been in
your bed you was out on the sand there schreechin' like
a pair of unredeemed catamounts. . . . Then *you*, Mr.
Dwyer, takes and carries her upstairs, with the pair of yez
drippin' like Tim Connel's ghost and him just after
drownin' himself for havin' hit Father Mulligan a skelp

77

wid an axe." Alanna, and 'tis with a sigh of relief and the divil's own skippin' of pages that you finally claw your way out of the tunnel of love.

The culmination of "Wife of the Centaur" may be one of the mildest in letters, but I was never so glad to see a culmination in my life. It is, of course, Inez, the girl with the chameleon eyes, who motivates it; Jeffrey has barely settled down on a Connecticut hilltop with his bride when the enchantress slinks back into the plot and everything goes haywire again. Night after night, the harassed poet patrols the countryside, waging a losing fight against her allure and addressing rhetorical questions to the heavens: "Must all true metal be tempered in flame? Is every birth a long agony? *Designer infinite. . . . Ah! must Thou char the wood ere Thou canst limn with it?*" Then, at very long last, comes blessed deliverance for all hands. Amid melting snows and adjectives, Jeffrey finds that the dross has burned away, and in a single burst of renewed creativeness composes two hundred and sixty lines of a saga called "The Brook." "God, Joan! I've never written anything like it in my life before! It's poetry . . . it's great poetry!" But whether it is or not will forever rest a secret, because at this juncture the reader is swept up on a mountainous comber boiling with allusions to Botticelli, Pallas Athene, and the old surefire thunder of centaur hoofs, and is washed up, weak as a kitten, in the end papers.

THE REACTION of a forty-five-year-old stomach to twenty-five-year-old brandy is a physiological certainty, but surprisingly little information exists on how that organ responds to novels of the same vintage. My subsequent history, therefore, may have a trifling clinical value. For thirty-six hours after completing "Wife of the Centaur," I experienced intermittent queasiness, a tendency to howl "I'm a Philistine!" and an exaggerated revulsion for the printed page. A day or two later, while emptying a wheelbarrow of old books into a gully near my home, I saw (or thought I saw) a stout, bearded individual with four feet chasing a scantily clad maenad along a ridge. I returned home on the double and, having notified the local game warden, busied myself with indoor matters. Ever since, I have been hearing reedy sounds from the ridge, as of someone playing a rustic set of pipes. More than likely, the game warden got himself mixed up in a three-handed saturnalia and they're looking for a fourth. One of these evenings, as soon as I can get myself shod, I really must gallop up there and see.

Personne Ici
Except Us Chickens

Yes, it was fantastic, inconceivable, illogical, but no more so than lots of things that happen nowadays. One sunny forenoon along about the middle of March, the man whose teeth I brush every morning (although there is less and less left to brush of late) was seated on the top step of a country post office in eastern Pennsylvania, immersed in a recent issue of *Harper's Bazaar*. It was a peaceful scene and one that would have quickened the step of any painter —the feathery pale green of the willows mirrored in the placid bosom of the canal, the darker green of the man's face suspended above the magazine, the rainbow pastel of steam escaping from his nostrils as he warmed to its pages. I had just skimmed the Paris openings and was sampling an essay on estrogenic face creams when Rufe Hillpot slid down beside me. Rufe is a fibrous little poultryman of sixty-odd whose solvency is as questionable as that of Prudential Life and who has forgotten more about baby chicks than *Harper's Bazaar* will ever know. Not that this sleek publication ordinarily concerns itself with anything so mundane, but spread out on the page before me was a photograph of seven cheeping Leghorn chicks pecking straw, seductively captioned "And Even the Chickens Work for Beauty."

"What's that book?" demanded Rufe, professional curiosity finally conquering his deep-rooted conviction that anything in print is a ruse to extract money from the unwary. I told him it was a gazette of the bon ton chiefly devoted to feminine fashion and Milady's loveliness. "You read that?" he asked with a quick, suspicious glance. "Why?"

"Well—er—I like to look at the patterns," I said lamely, and then flushed scarlet. "I mean my wife's in the garment trades—that is, she trades one garment for another—" Fortunately, Rufe's interest had shifted to the photograph of the chicks, and I hastily followed up the advantage. "Listen to this, Rufe," I said with a deep, booming laugh that scotched any hint of androgyny. "Right up your alley." I read off the caption to him in a manly bass. "'All Paris is talking about a new beauty product called Retzoderme that is supposed to be death on wrinkles. "It comes from chickens," women scream to each other over the lunch table, and so it does, for its manufacturers call it an embryonic juice extracted from eggs at the moment when the embryo's cells are reproducing most rapidly. It is sealed in glass ampoules and rushed, fresh, to the lady's dressing table. Parisiennes swear that they can see results after only a few days' use, especially on the crêpy skin of the neck. The Leghorn farm and laboratory where the product is made is on the outskirts of Paris near the Forest of Marly. And there we photographed these baby chicks destined for a long career of egg-laying solely in the interests of beauty. Sorry, there's no Retzoderme in America —as yet.' "

"You know," remarked Rufe, thoughtfully rubbing his grizzled chin, "if a feller played his cards right, that could turn into a nice sideline."

"Darn tooting," I said, humoring him. "A hatchery the size of yours, he'd be on Easy Street in no time. Of course, he'd have to nip over to the old country and see how they do it."

"You hit the nail on the head, son," said Rufe. "When do we start?"

"Now, hold your horses, Rufe," I said indulgently. "You don't really believe this works, do you?"

"Why not?" he snapped. "Says so in the paper, don't it?"

"Sure, sure," I said, "but you've got to understand about the cosmetic industry." I made a short, incisive talk, not one word of which he heard, explaining how the journalistic peony thrives in the rich humus of publicity and advertising, and, at the end of it, reluctantly consented to lend him the magazine overnight. There was a feverish glint in his eye when I dropped him off at his barn, and I did not like the glib *"Oui, m'zoo"* with which he acknowledged my parting injunction to stick to his last.

EARLY THE NEXT MORNING, as I was cross-pollinating the ageratum (I always like to cross-pollinate the ageratum before the linnets get into it), Rufe excitedly sped up the lane in his Winton Six and collared me. His kin had discussed the commercial potentialities of the rejuvenator and were prepared to underwrite an immediate trip abroad to scout its validity and production technique. They felt, furthermore, that if I could be persuaded to accompany Rufe, my familiarity with France would be invaluable in smoothing his way.

"Won't cost you a dime," he said forcefully. "All expenses paid—in a thing as big as this, a man can't afford to be a piker. Just say the word and I'll phone down to Philly for the plane tickets."

"Wait a minute, friend," I protested. "I wouldn't mind a week or two in Paris, but I've got a family to think of."

"It'd be a marvellous rest for them while you're gone," he pointed out coaxingly. "Tell you what, I'll throw in a Maggy Rouff ensemble for the Missis. How's that?"

"You're certainly picking up the idiom fast," I commented.

"I always keep abreast of the times," Rufe said coolly. "Well, what's the verdict—yes or no?"

"Jeekers!" I began, my thoughts in a whirl. "You act

as if this were a trip to Allentown. You'd have to get a passport and—"

Rufe looked over his shoulder at a pair of robins scrutinizing us narrowly from a nearby herbaceous border and lowered his voice. "I know a Red in the State Department who can fix anything," he confided. "Now, how much applejack will we need?"

The task of justifying a spontaneous trip overseas to my wife was not easy, but once she grasped the importance of our errand and the magnitude of the stakes involved, her misgivings vanished. The realization that she would have a free hand with the household chores, the dishwashing and scrubbing that I had selfishly appropriated as my special domain, more than compensated for the crêpes Suzette and vintage champagne I was slated to enjoy. Chief among the problems confronting Rufe and me in the hurly-burly of leave-taking was the question of wardrobe. It was my colleague's opinion, and I heartily concurred, that our native overalls and galluses would excite derision in the *beau monde;* we wished, understandably, to mingle inconspicuously on soigné levels without the imputation of "hayseed" being thrown at us. I therefore procured, after some searching, a couple of Prince Albert coats and silk toppers with conical crowns, of the sort worn by those legendary stereotypes, Alphonse and Gaston. The effect was Frenchy in the extreme, and it was obvious from the deference with which everyone at Idlewild gave way to us that we would have no difficulty in passing as *flâneurs* just off the Grand Boulevards.

TWENTY-THREE hours after the moment the giant airliner soared up from the runway, Rufe and I were seated before Byrrh-cassis at Fouquet's, on the Champs-Elysées, our eyes drinking in the colorful panorama eddying about us. Ever and anon, saucy midinettes with hatboxes twinkled past, their silken ankles a target for the ardent glances of gendarmes twirling spiked mustaches and muttering appreciative ooh-la-las. Flower-sellers hawked their wares—i.e., sold their flowers—amid the undulating throng; furtive apaches from Montmartre in gooseneck sweaters and caps, bent on who knows what sinister missions, slunk by, now and then violently repulsing their importunate drabs; and everywhere on the terrace elegantly gowned women in the latest creations from Paris flaunted their plumage and shrilly exchanged beauty recipes.

"You don't see anything like this in Plumsteadville, do you?" I observed jokingly. "Keep your ears open, Rufe; if that chicken juice is really meritorious, these gals'll know the score." Hardly had the words left my lips when I heard a high-pitched feminine voice behind me. "*Ça vient des poulets!*" it was screaming. "It comes from chickens! It's *merveilleux, épatant, incroyable!*" I nudged Rufe significantly and we craned around to obtain a better view of the speaker. She was a handsome *femme du monde* in her early forties, superbly hatted, gloved, and shod by the most exclusive couturiers of the Rue de la Paix, and every detail, from her heaving embonpoint down to her diavolo heels, was a testimonial to Gallic

85

chic. She had distended the erstwhile crêpy skin of her neck for the inspection of her companion, an equally modish lady, and was exhibiting the miraculous change wrought by the ampoule before them on the table. "But eet ees like suède, *votre peau* [your skin]!" the other woman exclaimed rapturously, unscrewing a watchmaker's glass from her eye. "*Ma foi*, this unparalleled extract of embryonic fowls should prove a boon to countless women which they are distraught by crow's-feet and similar inroads of senility!"

"You hear that?" whispered Rufe triumphantly. "I bet this is going on all over town, like the paper said." And, indeed, loath as I was to spring to conclusions, a circuit of various haunts of fashion—the Steam Room of the Ritz, Weber's, the Crémaillère, and the Ambassadeurs—corroborated his belief. Wherever smart society foregathered, the magic wrinkle-remover was the topic of the moment; Dior and Balenciaga, quick to sense a trend, had seized on poultry as the leitmotiv of their spring collections, and "Cracked Corn," the nude revue at the Bal Tabarin, was in its eighth smash week. Satisfied that *Harper's Bazaar* had not exaggerated the furor caused by the cream, Rufe proposed that we address ourselves to the task of eliciting its formula. He was all for a bold frontal attack, suggesting that we invade the laboratory, lay our pasteboards on the table, and negotiate for American manufacturing rights. The time had now come, I felt, to reveal to my partner the fruit of certain inquiries I had been developing privately.

"Rufe," I said, choosing my words carefully, "you must first be apprised that the White Russian syndicate that controls this process—former Czarist officers and unscrupulous men, as you will shortly comprehend—has no earthly intention of relinquishing a secret worth, by conservative estimate, many millions of francs. Worse yet, by approaching them as you indicate, you will fall into the very trap they have prepared for you."

"What's that? What's that?" he exclaimed agitatedly. "Do they know we're here?"

"Know?" I permitted myself a thin smile. "They *lured* you here, man. What if I were to tell you that they printed that one special copy of *Harper's Bazaar*, with its caption designed to inflame your poultryman's cupidity, just to entice you away from Pennsylvania?"

"But—but I don't follow," Rufe faltered. "Why should they do that?"

"So they could buy your hatchery at a fraction of its value," I said. "They desperately needed your chicks and your reputation to capture the American market, and with a ruthlessness unmatched in modern criminal annals, they will stick at nothing to attain their ends. Here is a cable from your son, who fortunately did not yield to the blandishments of their agents and wired me in time."

"I knew there was suthin' fishy from the start," said Rufe slowly. "When did you cotton on to these sarpints?"

"When I detected one of their creatures tailing us from Orly airport," I replied. "This morning, while you were still in the arms of Morpheus, I drove to the Forest of

Marly, entered the laboratory by forcing a sash, and established their guilt from the documents hidden in a disused autoclave."

"I'll teach those plausible Rooshians to trifle with a Yankee farmer," he declared, bristling like a turkey cock. "We're taking the next plane."

"Steady on, Rufe," I calmed him. "We can still turn the tables and get that formula, if you've nerve enough. Listen . . ."

FOUR HOURS LATER, the two of us crouched in the bedroom closet of a luxurious apartment on the Avenue Hoche tenanted by Gaby Delorme, the star of "Cracked Corn" and reigning toast of Paris. In a few terse whispers, I sketched in complexities I had hitherto withheld from my companion—how Grimalkin, head of the White Russian syndicate and Gaby's lover, had been deceiving the fair songstress with other women and how, by cleverly playing on her jealousy, I had influenced her to betray the formula to us.

"Why can't she betray it to us on the phone?" asked Rufe querulously. "What fer do we have to skulk in here like a passel of raccoons?"

"Sh-h-h!" I cautioned. "That's the way things are done over here." Applying my eye to the keyhole, I made out Grimalkin, tipsily sprawled on a chaise longue, downing repeated goblets of Pol Roger while the beauteous Gaby, in a revealing peignoir, murmured endearments in his ear. The Muscovite's tongue was loosened and it was manifest that he was on the point of divulging the information we sought when events took a singularly unexpected turn. A peremptory knock sounded at the bedroom door and Gaby sprang up, her face ashen.

"*Mon Doo,* my 'usband!" she gasped. "If 'e finds you 'ere, *chéri,* 'e weel keel you!"

"Name of a name!" exploded Grimalkin. "Why have I never heard of this husband before?"

"Ze exposition was too extensive to plant 'is existence," she hissed. " 'Ide queek—no, not under ze bed; in ze closet!" Before Rufe and I could scramble behind the racks of costly gowns and furs, the closet door flew open and Grimalkin landed in our midst. I clapped a hand over his mouth to prevent his crying out, but luckily the wine had fuddled his senses and after a brief, unavailing struggle he grew passive.

Aeons passed as we cowered there expecting momentary discovery and humiliation; then the door reopened softly and Gaby, in an expressive pantomime signifying that her husband was reassured, conducted Rufe and me to a waiting fiacre. What became of the sodden Grimalkin, I cannot state with certainty, though the fact that there was a second fiacre, waiting behind ours, spoke volumes for Gaby's resourcefulness. Indeed, eight or ten fiacres were standing by, and I wondered fleetingly what the rest of her closets contained, but in the bustle of departure I thought it best not to pry.

ONE WEEK AFTERWARD, I sat again on the top step of our rural Pennsylvania post office, idly watching the willow fronds sway in the warm breeze as I waited for the mail to be sorted. The benign sunshine had wafted me into semi-consciousness when an object similar to a rolled-up periodical dropped into my lap. As I straightened up with a start, I descried a familiar figure dwindling in the distance.

"Hi there, Rufe!" I sang after him. "What's your hurry, stranger? I never see you around any more!" He shouted something evasive about the egg business taking up most of his time. "Say, look here!" I called, holding up the newly arrived *Harper's Bazaar*. "Here's the latest issue of that magazine! Don't you want to borrow it?" To my surprise, he broke into a run as I started toward him, and vanished across the fields. I still can't figure out his motive; probably associated me with some frustration in his past, but Lord knows what. I tell you, just try and fathom these country people. *Ils sont absolument biscuit.* (They're absolutely crackers.)

Nirvana Small
by a Waterfall

WITH BARELY POTABLE SPIRITS fetching a king's ransom these days, and the price of barbiturates indistinguishable from that of gold dust, it ought to interest anyone looking for a little fast surcease that the best fifteen-cent nepenthe in town is still Louella Parsons' monthly column in *Modern Screen*. Slick though the testimonial may sound, I have been using the lady's feed-box gossip (in moderation, naturally) over the past twelvemonth and I can honestly say that it has been a boon. Once your system adjusts to her syntax, and the initial impulse to scream or scale a tree wears off, it has a wonderfully emollient effect, somewhat like sliding into a tub of lukewarm oatmeal. It slows down the heartbeat to turtle pace, irons out those corduroy furrows in the forehead, and sets up a pleasurable tingling in the Malpighian layer. I cannot for the life of me understand why the medical profession has shown no inclination to adopt it as an all-purpose anodyne. True, the back numbers of the *National Geographic* in the general practitioner's waiting room have an undeniably narcotic value, but for a real charge Lollie stands alone. The next time you feel prompted to bolt to your healer, seek out the nearest newsstand. You don't even need a prescription.

The title of the column, "Louella Parsons' Good News," is a largely arbitrary designation; most of the glad tidings seem to consist of tempestuous divorces and the unerring instinct of Homo Hollywood to mismate. "What a month of headlines!" exclaims the fair conductress, opening her March article with a catalogue of current rifts in the households of Barbara Stanwyck, Elizabeth Taylor, and Judy Garland. "Whew! Never can I remember so many important stories from movietown breaking so close together—and, frankly, never can I remember working so hard batting out my scoops and 'inside' yarns on wot hoppen." An appealing vignette this, the veteran hunched over her typewriter in the turbulent city room, eyeshade askew and corncob ablaze, pecking out bulletins and gulping coffee from a cardboard container. Not all of Louella's dispatches, to be sure, are couched in such breakneck Hildy Johnson tempo; she normally favors a gelatinous, sorghum-sweetened idiom in which archness, bonhomie, and vinegar struggle for mastery. Her antennae are quick to detect subterranean marital discord or the broken heart skillfully concealed. Last September, for instance, she remarked clairvoyantly, "I can't help feeling that Joan Fontaine is unhappy. Yes, I know she is a famous actress with beautiful clothes, admiring fans, a lovely home—all that goes with stardom. But, everytime I see her she seems so wistful. It is also my idea," she continued, displaying her matchless talent for sucking honey from nonexistent flowers, "that she is NOT carrying a torch for good-looking agent, Charlie Feldman, her ex-husband Bill Dozier, or any other gent." A cast into troubled waters the previous April brought forth another cupcake frosted with custard and strychnine. Commenting on Jennifer Jones' renewed radiance since marrying David Selznick, she observed, "During their engagement, they battled continually and usually staged their biggest tiffs at parties. One or the other of them would leave in a huff. But at Nadya and Reggie's [a buffet supper *chez* Reginald Gardiner], all was sweetness and light between the Selznicks." Evidently this heavenly rapport acted like wine on the correspondent, for the same party produced two added sugar-plums. Joan Bennett, she reported, "was saying she spent a fortune educating her daughter—who is now using that education to raise grapes in Imperial Valley! 'She is happiest,' said Joan, referring to Diana, her eldest, married daughter —'when dashing about in a red jeep, seeing how the grapes are coming on.'" Of the state of the grapes—whether they had agreed to disagree—there was no indication; forthwith, the spotlight turned on Mrs. Tyrone Power: "Linda Christian Power, who dramatizes everything, gave us a blow-by-blow account of her robbery in Mexico City—and what a difficult time her brother's wife had when her baby was born. All the time the fascinating and volatile Linda was telling us these tidbits, she was also modelling her new Italian gown and showing us her French purse—the latter giving me an idea. I have a top just like the little jade mouse on her handbag that I could use as a clasp—only my top is composed of elephants." Under these booming non sequiturs, hypertension falls away, the reader's jaw relaxes, and he is transported, beyond reach of internal revenue and nuclear fission, onto the seventh astral plane.

If I were bullied into choosing the story in which Miss Parsons comes closest to artistry, I would vote unhesitatingly for her report, this March, of starlet Ruth Roman's adventures in housekeeping with her husband, Mortimer Hall:

> Ruth met Morty when she was in New York last September. She was lunching at "21" Club with a girl friend who introduced her to the good-looking young millionaire sitting at an adjoining table. "So you are Ruth Roman," said the handsome gent she was to marry within three months. "I'm coming to the Coast soon to manage my mother's network out there. (His mother is Mrs. Dorothy Schiff, publisher of the New York *Post* and owner of KLAC radio station.) I was told to look you up.". . . A few days after they returned from their 24-hour honeymoon Morty said to her: "How much money do you need to run the house?" "Money?" said Ruth. "I don't need it. I can take care of the household expenses." "Not on your life," said the head of the family, shoving a wad of bills into her hand. "I'M paying all the bills. You're a married woman now, baby."

After he bolted out the door, Ruth just sat there and cried. . . . Morty also insisted that Ruth move out of her house and into his. He is firmly convinced that a wife shouldn't remain in the domicile where she has lived as a bachelor girl. Nobody knows this—but Ruth's "wonderful guy" is so sold on this idea—he wouldn't even move in her house for the few days she needed to pack and move out. For three days—the newlyweds lived in separate houses! The reason Ruth couldn't move in immediately is that she has two dogs and two cats—and a runway had to be fixed at Mr. Hall's house before Mrs. Hall could move in with her private zoo.

THE TRIALS AND TRIBULATIONS of the Halls in launching their matrimonial bark are doubly absorbing because they parallel, in many respects, those of Rhonda St. Cyr and Stewart Fels-Natchez, another pair of newly-weds in the screen colony. Miss St. Cyr, it will be recalled, played the role of the pretty hourglass vender in "Fly by Noon" and the lady neurologist in "Schizoids Three," and her madcap elopement to Las Vegas with the playboy Ohioan set the film capital by the ears. The following playlet, based on tape recordings made by friends after their return, as a post-nuptial gift, might be dubbed a semi-documentary. However dubbed, it is an indisputable slice of life and, in common with all organic matter (including gossip columns), should be kept in a refrigerator until ready to serve.

SCENE: *The living room of Stewart Fels-Natchez's palatial salt box in Beverly Hills. The basic décor is Arabian*

*and, to judge from the quantity of massive earthenware
jars on view, might easily be the headquarters of Ali Baba,
but the Pennsylvania Dutch dough tray and spatter floor,
Queen Anne highboy, and chromium bar upholstered in
okapi hide proclaim its owner a connoisseur who can afford to indulge his taste. Bookshelves filled with priceless
literary treasures—Avon, Bantam, the cream of the world's
great abridgments—also stamp him an inveterate reader.
As the curtain rises, Pargeter, a dignified English manservant in butler's apron, is surprised before the fireplace
consigning an armload of cabinet photographs to the
flames and brushing up the exposition.*

PARGETER (*aloud*): Ah, well, there's the last of the
master's youthful indiscretions, bless him for a high-spir-
ited colt. Now that connubial bliss is his, you—ahem!—
young persons will only foul up the premises, so away
with you. They do say that ever since Mr. Stewart met
Miss St. Cyr, he's forsworn his fliggertigibbet ways. I don't
doubt she'll be the making of the boy. Hello—I think I
hear his supercharged Alfa-Romeo crunching up the driveway. This is where I scuttle off belowstairs, so as not to
be under the feet of the doting honeymooners. (*He exits.
The door opens boisterously, and Stewart strides in, bearing Rhonda in his arms. There is a sheen about them.*)

RHONDA (*gazing about, enraptured*): Stooky! It's di-
voon!

STEWART: Like it, lover?

RHONDA: Oh, lambie, leave me down out of your importunate arms, as I must browse around and drink my

fill of everything. (*Clapping her hands*) An aquarium! How darling! Here, fishie-fishie!

STEWART: They don't know you yet. I mean you're still a stranger to them.

RHONDA: You watch, we'll be friends in no time. I'm a regular bug on ichthyology.

STEWART: Queer, I sort of sensed it. When two persons are very deeply in love, sometimes they can commune without words.

RHONDA: I wish I could express myself like you. I think that's what first enthused me anent a certain Mr. Stewart Fels-Natchez. That and the funny, crinkly laughter lines around his eyes.

STEWART (*ardently*): Gee, I could gobble you up in one bite!

RHONDA: Now, stop it, naughty boy, you're loosening all the cherries on my hat. Is that our pool out there in the patio?

STEWART: No, that's the servants' pool. Ours is in the bedroom upstairs.

RHONDA (*looking up*): Doesn't it leak down through the plaster?

STEWART: Uh-uh. I had tar paper laid between the beams.

RHONDA: You shouldn't have went to all the expense, precious.

STEWART: Well, after all, it would sting a chap's pride to have his snookums laying down here with moisture dripping on top of her unruly head.

RHONDA: Honest, I sometimes think you must be a

Latin to understand women the way you do. (*They kiss hungrily.*) What is that strange crisscross door sawed in the wall there?

STEWART: Never mind, you will be apprised in due course. First off, how are you fixed for cash to run our domicile?

RHONDA: Oh, I have scads. We mummers earn a goodly stipend, you know.

STEWART: Silly, impractical angel! Henceforward, Madam, I foot the bills and no sass. Here is a bundle of scratch to grease the skids, and should you at any time need largess for the bird that delivers the bottled water or so, simply let out a holler.

RHONDA (*through a mist of tears*): Nobody ever had such a thoughtful hubby. Prince Charming was an ignatz alongside of you.

STEWART: Your lips set my brain on fire—

RHONDA (*evading him*): But I don't think you really trust me, else you would wise me up as to the function of that door.

STEWART: Don't be nosy, honey. Remember what happened to Mrs. Bluebeard.

RHONDA: If you hadn't been so nosy at the Sump Room in Chicago, we wouldn't of met. I was eating a *shashlik* off a flaming spear and you couldn't keep your eyes off me.

STEWART: You know why? The night prior, I caught your personal appearance at the Mastbaum in Philly, and you were alike as two peas. It was fantastic.

RHONDA: I'll never forget when my secretary introduced

us. You said, "So this is Rhonda St. Cyr. Well, my old man has more kale than anybody in Ashtabula. He's got bakeries and lubritoriums and wet-wash laundries, and I'm going to lavish it all on you.

STEWART (*fondly*): Was that when you definitely started to care?

RHONDA: No. I could never be taken by storm. I was intrigued when you did over that Glendale theatre lobby in chinchilla for my preview.

STEWART: I had a trick idea the time you went to Honolulu. I was going to rent a Piper Cub to strew orchids on your ship over the Golden Gate.

RHONDA: I'm glad you didn't. I hate garishness. (*Pouting*) Stooky, dear, mayn't I have just one bitty peek behind that door?

STEWART (*relenting*): Oh, well, you were bound to sooner or later. (*Opening it*) It's a runway.

RHONDA: (*ecstatically*): A *runway!*

STEWART: Yes, for your private zoo. Knowing your oft-expressed kinship for your animal chums, I moved mountains to bring them in arm's reach. Come on, fellows! (*A puma, closely followed by a gibbon and a llama, plummet in and leap distractedly about their mistress.*)

RHONDA (*cuddling them joyfully*): Did ever a bride's cup brim over like yours truly's? Sweetheart, I fear it's some marvellous golden dream.

STEWART: Your woman's intuition tells you true. Who do you think is lodged in this closet, biding my signal to erupt on the scene?

RHONDA: My—my numerologist?

99

STEWART: No, our lawyers. (*Soberly*) Rhonda, we must be brave. Our marriage has drifted on the rocks. The both of us are living a lie.

RHONDA (*dully*): I—felt something had snapped, too.

STEWART: Ever since our union forty-eight hours ago, I sensed it was doomed. Deep down, you rebelled against my dating other bimbos and squiring them to the niteries.

RHONDA: It's nobody's fault, Stewart. People with careers like ours aren't fated to love.

STEWART: You'll always remain a shrine in my memory. No matter how many ears I whisper sweet nothings in, your dear face will rise to haunt me.

RHONDA: Likewise, darling. (*Her voice breaks.*) If only—oh, if only Louella or Hedda Hopper were here to share our unhappiness!

STEWART: They are, dearest—and Skolsky, too. (*Neatly synchronized with his words, the celebrated trio rise from the earthenware jars at rear, whisk open notebooks, and clamor for details of the property settlement, division of yachts, etc. Rhonda silences them with a gesture.*)

RHONDA: One moment, please. We want you three to be the first to know. We're going on a second honeymoon. We've found each other again. (*Sensation*) Thanks to a loyal mate which he was tireless to anticipate my every wish, we have wrote finis to conjugal strife. In her next vehicle, the fans will see a new, more mature Rhonda St. Cyr, mellowed by suffering and compassion.

STEWART (*softly*): To be followed, I may divulge, by a chubby little sequel, with Stewart Fels-Natchez, quondam playboy, listed as the associate producer.

Nirvana Small by a Waterfall

PARSONS, HOPPER, AND SKOLSKY (*exhaling*): Judas Priest, what a story! (*As they scatter to alert the wire services, the couple embrace, the gibbon showers them with confetti, the puma lies down with the llama, and the lawyers quietly smother in the closet.*)

CURTAIN

The Song Is Endless,
but the Malady Lingers On

HEAVEN KNOWS, nobody wants to bring the whole medical profession down around his ears like a swarm of B_1, and yet, judging from a couple of indications that have filtered through to me recently, I may have to tie up the old family physician and fall back on herbs and simples. I realize that in saying so I am deliberately courting a scalpel between the ribs in a dark alley; nevertheless, it looks as if the layman might well brace himself against some sizzling surprises that the boys in the crisp white tunics are preparing. It might be a very good idea not to swallow any chicken bones until the emergency passes, and if a cinder lodges in your eye, get your neighborhood jeweller to extract it. Personally, I intend to ask my insurance counsellor whether he can't rig up a temporary floater to protect me against Dr. Kildare during the next few months. Nothing elaborate, just some sort of medical collision-and-proximity damage to keep the healers away.

The first inkling of what lies in store for the unwary patient comes from a report, in the New York *Times*, of a recent meeting of the New Jersey Medical Society. At the close of the session, the members were presented with three-minute hourglass egg timers as ammunition in an all-out fight against socialized medicine. Directions for their use ran as follows:

> Place the timer on your desk in the consulting room. When the patient enters, up-end the glass without offering an explanation for your actions. After approximately three minutes, the sand has run through the glass and the consultation usually will have just begun. At this point explain to the patient that had he or she been in England or had we socialized medicine here, the consultation would be over. Another application of the plan is by way of showing that socialized medicine in the United States, based on an estimate of $15,000,000,000 per year, would cost $90,000 for the period it takes the sand to run through the timer.

An admirable propaganda scheme, especially with the patient paying admission to the lecture; all it lacks is the added refinement, overlooked by its sponsors, that he supply free sand as well. A further intimation that tempests may lurk in the path of the laity henceforward is contained in an article by Brian P. Flanagan, M.C., in the *Current Medical Digest* for March. Making a plea for more interesting case histories, the author urges doctors to couch their medical narratives in a vigorous literary style, to combine drama with clarity and conciseness. He furnishes three samples, the second of which demands quotation at some length to do it justice:

Name of Patient: John Everyman.
Age: 39.
Operation: Appendectomy.
Operative Note: Nervous and distraught, Emily paced up and down the sterile, comfortless hospital waiting room. Would John love her after the operation as much as he had before? She had been a good and faithful wife. What about Cecelia Bronson—that calculating, scheming scrub nurse? Emily knew that Cecelia was after John's money and would stop at nothing to get John away from her. In her distraught mind Emily could picture Cecelia up there in the operating room—her smooth cold face half-hidden by a surgical mask, her soft but cold eyes watching the operation as the white robed surgeon made the usual McBurney's incision, separated the muscles transversely in layers and exposed the peritoneum. She could hear his slow regular breathing as John lay unconscious while the anesthetist watched the pentothal oxygen and curare. She could see the flashing Kelly clamps as the appendiceal blood vessels were clamped and sutured, as the appendix was clamped, ligated, touched with phenol and inverted with a purse-string suture. She could see Cecelia handing the surgeon the sutures as the peritoneum and muscles were closed in layers with double 0 chromic catgut and the skin closed with B.S.S. What would it mean to John that Cecelia was there in this moment of suffering, while she—his own wife—was forced to wait, nervous and distraught in the waiting room? "Patient returned to room in good condition," the chart would read—yes, his body in good condition, but what about his heart? Would it still belong to her—post-op?

The Song Is Endless, but the Malady Lingers On

It is hard to foretell what impact the suggestions put forward by the New Jersey Medical Society and Dr. Flanagan will have on the average practitioner; the impact on the average patient—specifically, me—is numbing. Under the rosiest conditions, a visit to the doctor's office is no picnic, and I suspect that these Gothic touches, if they meet with professional favor, may transform it into a tolerably bloodcurdling experience. In the absence of formal laboratory equipment, I have been steeping the potentialities in an old earthenware crock sutured to the top of my spinal column and have distilled a vignette that outlines the dimensions of the problem:

CRYSTAL LAIDLAW snapped the elastic over the cover of her stenographer's notebook, tucked back a ribbon on her starched nurse's cap, and, smothering a yawn, peered furtively at her wristwatch. Inured as she was to the eccentricities of Dr. Fergus Culpepper, his growing tendency to interrupt dictation and hash over his literary output with colleagues on the phone was fast undermining her. The morning before, ignoring an anteroom full of patients, he had wasted a full half hour recapitulating to Trefflich, the orthopedist, the stirring disposition he had made of a fractured tibia. Trefflich, not to be outdone, had countered with an effort of his own provisionally dubbed "The Adventures of a Clavicle," in which a collarbone detailed the sensations attendant upon its owner's being flung off a motorcycle. To Crystal, fidgeting restlessly in her chair, the two sounded like a pair of journalism majors in Schrafft's recalling their themes and exulting over purple passages. Now her employer was off again, she noted with despair, this time on the saga he had composed about Mrs. Wainwright's dyspepsia.

"Of course, I knew it was only heartburn from the start, Ned," he was explaining volubly into the mouthpiece. "Cripes, you'd have to be a Zola to get any conflict or characterization out of a puny subject like that. Well, just as I was at my wit's end, the patient laid the plot right in my lap—got up in the middle of the night for bicarbonate, missed her footing, and rolled down a flight of stairs. . . . No, merely a few contusions, worse luck. . . . Well, anyway, it gave me the story line I was desperate for, and everything fell into place. Want to hear a dynamite opening? Get this: 'Writhing with pain whose origin was clearly psychosomatic, Emma Wainwright tossed about in her disordered bed. In her equally disordered mind, there was no vestige of pity for the luckless husband tossing beside her, or for the long-suffering physician she was about to awaken and plague with her symptoms.' Pretty suspenseful stuff, what? . . . Well, I haven't decided yet, but *Argosy's* clamoring for it and I promised to let them have first crack. How's that pancreas serial coming along? . . . Splendid. See you soon." He hung up, and his face, as he swivelled back toward Crystal, was creased by a frown. "Jealous old dodo," he said testily. "He knows I can write rings around him. Oh, well . . . Where'd we leave off?"

"You were just comparing Mr. Folwell's liver to the

Rose Window at Chartres," replied his nurse. "But don't you think you'd better see Mr. Duveneck? He's been waiting outside almost an hour."

"Blast," growled Culpepper. "The minute I get really creative, these damn patients begin milling around here in droves. O.K., send him in." Reaching into a drawer, he brought forth an hourglass egg timer, an electric toaster, and a coffee percolater, which he ranged on the blotter before him. He was hacking off a slice of bread from a stale loaf when Duveneck, a pale, haggard man of forty with a day-old beard, sidled into the room nervously twisting his panama.

"Hello, Doc," he said, with a wan, conciliatory smile. "Gee, I didn't mean to interrupt your breakfast."

"You're not," Culpepper replied, upending the hourglass. "I ate it four hours ago."

"Then why are you setting up all those things? It looks as if—"

"Don't pry, Duveneck," the Doctor said severely. "Remember, curiosity killed a cat, and he was a lot nimbler than you, brother. Hmm, that's rather neat; may as well jot it down. I can use a nifty or two in that Folwell yarn to lighten it up. All right, now, what's ailing you?"

"Well, I'm not exactly sure," faltered Duveneck. "It started last night at my summer place up in Mahopac. You see, a fuse blew out and I went down cellar to fix it."

"Hold your horses," commanded Culpepper. "Stop right there. Do you realize," he asked impressively, holding up the egg timer between his thumb and forefinger, "that if

107

you and I were in England now, this interview would be over?"

"Why, yes," said his caller uncertainly. "It's five hours later over there than it is here."

"So it is," said the Doctor, thunderstruck. "Blow me down. The Society didn't think of that when they dreamed up this hourglass to illustrate the wastefulness of socialized medicine."

"Is—is that what the toaster and percolator are for, too?" inquired Duveneck.

"Search me," admitted the other. "I figured the idea needed some kind of production—window dressing, you might say. Well," he said, rising and extending his hand, "so long, and remind me to try out the patter on you the next time you come in. I'll have the right answers by then."

"But listen," protested Duveneck, "you haven't even heard my story."

"Something about a fuse, wasn't it?" observed the Doctor perfunctorily. "Here, take two of these capsules before each meal; the tingling ought to subside in about three days. How's Mrs. Duveneck?"

"Look, Doc," pleaded Duveneck, piteously indicating the crown of his head. "A whole carton of Mason jars fell off the shelf on me. I've got a lump the size of a walnut— it might be a concussion—"

"Nonsense," said Culpepper brusquely. "It's only a little tertiary swelling, nothing to speak of. You don't expect me to base a readable case history on that, do you?"

"No, but couldn't you just feel it and give me an opinion

or something?" Duveneck implored. "I wouldn't tell any-body, I promise."

"I'm afraid not, old man." The Doctor's lips compressed into a thin line. "There *is* such a thing as medical ethics, you know. Now, if it was a colorful injury, a gunshot wound or whatnot, I'd be delighted to help—always pro-vided it had a good exciting background, naturally."

"Honest, our cellar'd make a peach of a setting, Dr. Culpepper," insisted Duveneck. "You could do a great job on all those cobwebs and dark corners. No kidding, it's the spookiest place you ever saw. They—they say it used to be a station on the Underground Railroad."

"Kind of an Edgar Allan Poe slant, eh?" pondered the Doctor, chewing thoughtfully on his pencil. "We-e-ll, it might be the basis for a short short, though hardly the way it stands. I'd have to rearrange most of the action and dialogue."

"Oh, sure, sure, whatever you say," said Duveneck quickly. "I mean if you'd rather lay it in the attic, where I knock my head against a rafter—"

"One moment, Duveneck," Culpepper interrupted, with hauteur. "I wasn't aware we were collaborating on this. I'm perfectly capable of handling it without any outside assistance."

"Of course you are," agreed the suppliant, cringing. "Gosh, I hate people who tell professionals how to write, don't you? Oh—er—to get back to this bump again—"

"There's no necessity to," said Culpepper crisply. "I'll probably use an entirely different motivation; I might de-cide to have you stumble over a shovel or wrench your back colliding with the furnace. The device is unimportant. What I've got to capture and convey to the reader is a man's panic and isolation at an instant of crisis." He sprang up and described a wide, sweeping gesture. "By George, I might even climax with you lying there slowly gasping out your life while scarcely fifteen feet away your wife rocks placidly over her knitting, unaware of your predicament. Think of that for irony!"

"I am—I mean I will," Duveneck assured him, "but in the meantime isn't there anything I could put on my head? It throbs something awful."

"Yes, try a cold poultice or a knife blade," said the Doctor indifferently. "And take my card. In case you fall down senseless in the street, I can be reached either here or at the Authors League." Picking up his patient's hat, he escorted him to the door. "Ta-ta, now," he said with an abstracted smile. "Drop in any old time." For a minute after Duveneck had gone, he stood absorbed in thought. Then he darted to his desk and dialled a number.

"Lucas?" he asked. "Fergus Culpepper. . . . First-rate, how are you? . . . Say, you once treated Hammerstein or Rodgers, I forgot which. . . . Yes, I *knew* I was right. . . . Well, could you arrange to introduce us? I've got a melodramatic musical comedy all worked out, and, if I do say so, it's a humdinger. . . . I know that, but do me a favor and listen to the first scene. It's the cellar of a Long Island mansion, see, and the owner, a chap on the order of Rex Harrison, has just left a very gay dinner party to replace a fuse. . . ."

CLOUDLAND REVISITED:

Oh, Sing Again
That Song of Venery

⊂≢

BACK IN THE SPRING of 1926, that idyllic period which
now seems to have been part of the Golden Age, there
throve midway along West Eighth Street, in Greenwich
Village, a restaurant known as Alice McCollister's. It had
a pleasant back-yard garden, where tweedy, artistic folk
were wont to breakfast on Sunday mornings, equably
discussing such avant-gardist tendencies as Foujita's painting, the novels of Floyd Dell, and the composographs of
Peaches Browning. Every once in a while, the Sabbath
peace veiling the premises would be fractured by a piercing clarinet arpeggio from above, and, looking up in
irritation, the patrons would perceive a strange figure

seated on the fourth-floor window sill of an adjoining building. His gaunt face was strikingly similar to that of George Arliss, an illusion he fostered by affecting the sort of monocle worn by the star of "The Green Goddess." His hair, luxuriant as a fat-tailed sheep's, hung low on his neck, and the visible portion of his body was clad in a Russian tunic decorated with red and blue cross-stitch. Braced in the window frame, his licorice stick wailing forth a freehand version of "Milenberg Joys," Hilary Tremayne would be notifying the world in his usual heterodox fashion that he was a free spirit. He would also be giving his three roommates, of whom I was the sleepiest, a persistent pain in the fundament.

Considering that we all shared a chamber roughly seventeen by twelve for six months, I knew relatively little about Hilary, but what little I knew was enough. An actor by profession, he had early adopted the name of Tremayne as a stylish variant of his own, which was, I believe, either Troutman or Appenzeller. His major acting triumphs had occurred south of Fourteenth Street, in Restoration comedies at the Cherry Lane, though on one occasion he had impersonated a faun in the Theatre Guild production of Franz Werfel's "The Goat Song." Currently, he was attending Richard Boleslavsky's school of the drama, and he was forever using terms like "dynamics," "spatial interplay," and "Aristotelian progression" to explain what went on behind the footlights. Guilfoyle and Froelich, the two other roommates, were the only members of our quartet with any semblance of a steady income. The former, a neat, bloodless youth, worked as bookkeeper at a stevedoring concern down around Bowling Green. He was engaged to a deeply devout girl in Brooklyn who disapproved of his bohemian associates, and, when he was not escorting her to vespers, which was seldom indeed, hovered before the mirror searching his alabaster skin for blemishes. Froelich, a salesman for household appliances and the Don Juan of the fraternity, was no older than the rest of us, but his excursions into a thousand boudoirs had given him a premature suavity and polish that, as he freely admitted, turned women's bones to water at a single glance. Ninety per cent of the incoming calls on our telephone were beamed at Froelich— lovelorn wives whose husbands were away on business trips and who thirsted for his ministrations, he said, with a self-deprecatory shrug, and patted his receding hairline. I often wondered why he stayed in the Village, since, like Guilfoyle's fiancée, he professed intense scorn for its crackpot literati and painters. One day, he enlightened me. He hoped to compose popular songs eventually, and felt he owed it to his muse to steep himself in a milieu charged with significant new rhythms. "Besides," he added pensively, "there's a lot of gorgeous quail in this section."

WAVE ON WAVE of such Proustian memories—well, if not waves, a needle shower—buffeted me the other day when, cropping through a Pennsylvania country library, I came across a copy of a book called "Leonie of the Jungle," by Joan Conquest. Miss Conquest's novel was one item of my spiritual pabulum in that remote era—the roast course, you might say. I read it at Froelich's recommendation (his literary taste was as catholic as his choice of bedfellows), and if it did nothing else, it at least spared me the expense of an electric heater those chilly spring evenings. Though I had long ago forgotten the background, characters, and plot, I distinctly remembered it as a lollapaloosa; even plucking the volume from the shelf produced a vague incandescence in my cheeks, comparable to the effect of a double Chartreuse. I stole a sidelong look at the librarian, nodding over her rubber stamps, and, with a quick, shoplifter's gesture, whipped it under my mackinaw. Whether it was guilt that made my heart pound all the way home or the evocative powers of the book, I cannot say for certain, but by the time I reached my own rooftree, I was in a lather of perspiration.

It began to dawn on me shortly after rereading a few pages that my crime was doubly heinous in that I had mulcted an object of no value whatever; far from robbing the library, in fact, I had unwittingly done a salutary job of scavenging. Somewhere over the past quarter century, the juice of the novel had calcified, or my nature had so coarsened that it derived very little moxie from the tale of an English girl's enslavement by a sinister Indian sect. Nevertheless, kleptomaniac and boor though I had become, I still had enough decency not to fling it aside with a snap judgment. Lighting up a Murad to induce nostalgia, and greasing my face with butter to protect it from the burning prose, I wallowed into the text like a Channel swimmer leaving Cape Gris-Nez.

Oh, Sing Again That Song of Venery

THE HEROINE OF "Leonie of the Jungle" makes her curtsy to us at the age of seven in a locale largely unexplored in the fiction of the budding twenties—a psychoanalyst's office. An orphan afflicted with somnambulism and malevolent dreams, she has been brought to a Harley Street specialist named Sir Jonathan Cuxson by her aunt, Lady Susan Hetth. Leonie is a veritable dewdrop of a child, with opalescent, gold-flecked eyes and a lisp that would melt the glue out of a revolving bookcase. The mention of a possible jog on a pony, for instance, precipitates the following: " 'I can't wide astwide,' she sighed. "I haven't any bweeches. . . . But I can swim, an' jump in out of my depff. I learnt in the baff at the seaside!' " Inquiries by Sir Jonathan establish that an Indian nurse gained a strong ascendancy over Leonie during her babyhood in India and may even have endowed her with strange psychic potency. The latter supposition is confirmed at the Zoo, to which she is taken by Jan, the Doctor's son; she handles a ravening Bengal tiger at will, doubtless anesthetizing the beast with her dialogue. " '*Poor* tiger!' she was saying. 'I'm vewwy sowwy for you—I'm sure you're not so vewy, vewy wicked, an' if you will bend your head, I will stwoke you behind the ear same as I did Kitty.' " Thanks to a chicken-hearted social system that forbids euthanasia for people who talk this way, Leonie is permitted to grow up and go to boarding school, where she practices sleep-walking almost as intensively as her colleagues do field hockey. In consequence, she is considered rather odd, an estimate that has some physical justification also, for the author says of her hands that "the fingers were like pea-pods, long and slender and slightly dimpled." You could hardly expect anybody, let alone a group of teen-age girls, to warm up to an ambulatory mess of greens drifting around in the moonlight and chanting, "I make oblation . . . let the gods come well willing!" It's vewwy unnerving, reawwy.

Her schooling finished, Leonie settles down on the north Devon coast with her aunt and there is forced into wedding Sir Walter Hickle, a loathsome, baseborn blackmailer who has been preying on Lady Susan. The union is particularly odious because, before it takes place, Leonie has met Jan Cuxson again and fallen in love with him. Jan, now a physician carrying on his father's work, chances to spy her during a somnambulistic seizure in which she executes a voluptuous belly dance invoking Kali, the Indian goddess of death. He tries to convince her that she is not daffy, as the evidence would indicate, but simply the victim of long-range mesmerism from India, interlarding the diagnosis with feverish busses and appeals to marry him instead of Sir Walter. That Leonie should mulishly reject his suit when it is open and shut that they are unavoidably headed for the same ostermoor seems a shade quixotic. Still, Miss Conquest has two hundred pages of Oriental monkeyshines to vend, and no parenthetical smooching is going to upset her applecart. The marriage, therefore, takes place on schedule; Jan, unreconciled, departs for India to track down Leonie's incubus—presumably by advertising in the incubus column of the Bombay *Daily Mail*

—and en route receives the cheery news that Sir Walter has perished in a fire on his wedding night. This deft bit of author's convenience effectively preserves the heroine's virginity for the second half of the book, when it will be called upon to weather truly hideous ordeals, and now the real fireworks begin.

THE SVENGALI actually responsible for Leonie's trauma, it appears, is a prince's son named Madhū Krishnaghar, who by sorcery and incantation has been striving to lure her back to the Peninsula to serve as his plaything and as priestess to Kali. His fiendish magic prevails. A few weeks later, we join the bewitched maiden aboard a liner steaming up the Hooghly, sleepwalking thirteen to the dozen. Madhū, a charm boy resembling Ramon Novarro at his prime, has sneaked on at Colombo, and here is the vision he sees as she trips out on deck in her nightgown: "She made an arresting picture as she stood listening intently, her flimsy garment falling away from her shoulders, leaving the slender white back bare to the waist, while she held handfuls of the transparent stuff crushed against her breast, upon which lay a jewel hung from a gold chain. . . . Sweetly she laughed up into his face as she laid one little hand upon the great white cloak which swung from his shoulders, unaware that in moving her hand her own garment had slipped, and that her beauty lay exposed like a lotus bud before his eyes. She came so close that her bare shoulder touched the fine white linen, and the curves of her scarlet lips were but a fraction of an inch from his own; and her whispered words in the eastern tongue were as a flame to an oil well." Even across the gulf of twenty-five years, I can still remember the thread of saliva that coursed down Froelich's chin as he read the foregoing passage aloud to us. His carnal instincts, I suppose, had been so whetted on importunate housewives that he found the sweetmeat irresistible. Madhū Krishnaghar, while sorely beset, displays greater self-control: "No movement of his body, but he gave a jerk of his will-power which brought the veins out like whipcord on his forehead, and drove the nails deep into the palms of his hands." In this awkward condition, he is plainly in no shape to wreak his will of Leonie, and she disembarks unsullied at Calcutta, blissfully ignorant, like Clarissa Harlowe, that her virtue is about to undergo further titanic stresses.

For a while, all is fun and games. Leonie turns the heads of the local sahibs, who haven't seen a podful of fresh peas since leaving Gib; she comports herself splendidly on a tiger shoot; and she pitches some woo with Dr. Jan, who, of course, behaves with gentlemanly British restraint even though the vapor is whistling from his ears. In a scene where he holds her "crushed to the point of agony against him with his mouth upon the sweetness of her neck," the author grows rather tart because he doesn't assert himself more strongly. "Heavens!" she exclaims. "What fools some men can be with that jungle animal woman within their hands! . . . Good heavens, why didn't he take her in his arms and smother her up against his heart, or put a bag over her head, or failing the bag, put his hand before her eyes?" At any rate, bored with his spineless grazing on her neck and his namby-pamby proposals, Leonie succumbs to the magnetism being exerted on her by Madhū Krishnaghar and takes off on a sightseeing tour of Benares. In the cupola of a temple near the holy city, Madhū, ostensibly acting as her guide, slips her a goof ball that paralyzes her will, and uncorks a plethora of such incendiary phrases as "thou white doe," "thou virgin snow," and so forth. Leonie responds with an abandon that would shame a dish of junket: "Wave after wave swept her from head to foot, causing her body, untrammeled by whalebone, to tremble against his, and he loosened the white cloak and let it fall, holding her pressed to him in her thin silk dress, laughing down at her, delighting in her eyes, her mouth, her throat." Yet before the sparks she has generated can leap into a holocaust, Miss Conquest perversely stamps them out. "He had not the slightest intention of doing her any harm," she notes, pursing her lips into a prim line, "but with the whole of his vividly mature brain and virgin body, he delighted in the effect of the drug upon the woman he loved." In other words, just a fun-loving kid motivated by curiosity, like any adolescent with his first chemistry kit.

The gambol in the cupola, it soon transpires, is merely antipasto for a real shindig at the Praying Ghats, the sacred stairs fronting the Ganges. Here, under the malign influence of Kali, Madhū and Leonie dunk each other in the river, hemstitch their frames with daggers, and generally take advantage of every inch of platitude allowed by the postal laws.

As the pressure intensifies and ecstasy fogs the author's lens, Leonie enters what can only be described as a chronic state of near-ravishment: "Leonie lay still, unconscious of the sound and the subtle change creeping over the man who bent down to her, and who, high-caste, over-educated, overstrung, aflame with love and afire with the sensuality of his religion, slowly tightened his hand upon the gracious curves of the slender throat." This and ancillary didos culminate in a whopper of an orgy at an adjacent temple, from which Leonie is delivered with her camisole in ribbons but her chastity, *Gott sei Dank*, intact. By now, to be excessively blunt, the reader would cheerfully assent to the game's being called on account of darkness, Madhū awarded the trophy on a technicality, and the arena hosed down. Whatever Miss Conquest's deficiencies as a novelist, however, she has one inflexible tenet: She never gives short weight.

Jan Cuxson, we discover in a flashback, has not failed his beloved, and through all her vicissitudes has been hot on her scent. Comparatively hot, that is; at the moment, he lies prisoner, chained to a ring in the wall, in the very temple where Leonie was drugged. His captor is a fanatical old priest who forgets to feed him for days at a time and occasionally spits on him, but, like Madhū, isn't really a bad egg: "The fine old man had no intention of torturing the white man, he had merely bound him to the ring until his goddess should inspire him, her servant, with her wishes." Gramps, as one is tempted to dub him, reveals to Jan that he consecrated Leonie as a baby to the divinity and that she will ultimately fetch up at his altar to be sacrificed. To save excessive travel and assure himself of a ringside seat at the blowoff, Jan sensibly decides to sit tight and await developments. In due time, Madhū and Leonie descend on the district, pale with exertion, but still full of ginger. They have been skittering all over western Bengal, playing puss in the corner and exchanging speeches like "Thy mouth is even as the *bimba* fruit, which is warm and soft, and thy chin is like a mango stone, and thy neck like unto a conch shell which I encircle with both hands." If any prospective Ph.D. longs to investigate the role of the neck in erotic literature, he has a mine of source material in "Leonie of the Jungle." At all events, Leonie suddenly throws off Madhū's spell, realizes her degradation, and spurns his love; he, incensed, hands her over to the priest, and then, just as she is about to be skewered, relents and averts the sacrificial blade. Simultaneously, Jan bursts his bonds, and the over-wrought author caps her climax with the classic device for finishing any story, "the greatest earthquake that ever swept the Sunderbunds Jungle." Madhū and the priest, quite properly, are expunged—the latter, with true consideration, releasing Leonie from the hex with his dying breath— and the lovers clinch in the afterglow. "There has been a bit of an earthquake, dear," Jan discloses in reply to his affinity's questions, "and you got hit on the head by a piece of falling brick." Leonie, her opalescent, gold-flecked eyes like saucers, demands reassurance: "Where are we going to? Where are you taking me?" "To Devon, beloved," returns Jan, sealing her mouth with honest, Occidental-type kisses. "To Devon and happiness!"

THERE IS AN OLD SAYING in my part of Pennsylvania, and I wish I could convey its sonorous beauty in Pennsylvania Dutch, that he who filches library books is a *Schwein* and that unto him there will subsequently come a day of reckoning. I never dreamt what wisdom the adage contains or how swiftly vengeance would overtake my transgression. Barely had I lifted my head from the last page of the book when my collar button, released from the tension it had been under for the previous two hours, popped off and struck the reading lamp, shivering it to smithereens. The room was plunged in darkness, and as I sat there, stunned, a low, sepulchral, and extremely horrid voice addressed me. *"Ham abhi ate hai,"* it said foreboding. *"Ham abhi ate hai."* Which, as the least accomplished student of Hindustani knows, means "I come—I come." It might have issued from the Pennsylvania Library Association or from some recondite Indian deity, but I had no overpowering urge to inquire. With a bound, I lit out onto the lawn, where I could have plenty of room to rassle. I caught a hell of a cold, spent three days in bed, and still can't figure out a way to return the book gracefully. Has anybody got a reliable fence? Has anybody got a single suggestion or, for that matter, an iota of pity? Me, I've got nothing—just rhinitis, a first edition of "Leonie of the Jungle," and a podful of remorse.

A Girl and a Boy Anthropoid
Were Dancing

☙

THERE IS MANY a justly celebrated name in the pantheon of show business, but last Saturday, looking over a small pantheon I keep handy so I can get at it in a hurry, I was struck by one omission. In the subsection enshrining strip-teasers, I found no mention of Rozina Carlomusto. All the others were there: dazzling Lili St. Cyr, who electrified Las Vegas a while back by peeling down to the ultimate rosette, jettisoning that, and landing in quod, an exploit that boosted her salary to five thousand dollars a week; Sherry Britten of the flamboyant torso, sometimes likened to a human acetylene torch; the immortal Gypsy Rose, Georgia Sothern, Hinda Wasau, Margie Hart, Ann Corio, and others too numerous to list. But of Rozina not a whisper, not even a footnote to remind posterity of her sensational performance with a stuffed gorilla which made theatrical history two short months ago.

The exact nature of the lady's specialty is not altogether clear; it seems to have been a cross between jujitsu and a gavotte, from which her partner invariably emerged victor. The ensuing chaotic account of the act and its repercussions appeared in the New York *Daily News:*

> CALUMET CITY, ILL., Oct. 9 (UP)—Justice of the Peace Ted Styka today tossed out the case against dancer Rozina Carlomusto, accused of staging a lewd wrestling match with a stuffed gorilla in a night club. "Insufficient evidence," Styka ruled, even though authorities had claimed that Miss Carlomusto always lost the fall to the gorilla. The police said it appeared that the gorilla completed a seduction of the dancer during the act . . . It (the gorilla) is still in the hands of the State's Attorney's office as evidence. Last month the dancer gave a command performance in court so that Styka could judge for himself whether the act was "lewd and lascivious" as charged. She stripped to the bare essentials in chambers and went into an animated tussle with the stuffed beast. Sure enough, the gorilla won, pinning Rozina in 10 minutes flat. "This is a work of art," she said. "I've performed the same show hundreds of times in Panama and before soldiers in U.S.O. shows. This is the first time anybody questioned the dance."

What the poor, bewildered kid doesn't realize, of course, is that she is a victim of the same quidnuncs and busybodies who have plagued every artist from Zola and D. H. Lawrence to Joyce Hawley. Here is a girl quietly wrestling away with a gorilla in a spotlight, enriching the cultural life of her community and impinging on nobody's livelihood. You can depend on some salvation-happy bluenose, with a paid-up annuity in Paradise, to begin reading things into it. I don't want to borrow trouble, but once such folk get the upper hand, we are finished—*ausgespielt*. It will no longer be possible for your daughter and mine to disrobe on a night-club floor and juggle a pair of doves or plastic bubbles, and before you know it, all the calendars will be featuring depressing snow scenes and collies instead of voluptuous maidens in black net curled around a telephone. If we aren't heading into the most repressive era since Cromwell, I'm a Chinaman.

The thing that really riles me, though, is the aura of secrecy surrounding Rozina's demonstration in court. We are told that "she stripped to the bare essentials in chambers and went into an animated tussle with the stuffed beast." Does Mr. Styka suppose for a moment that he can dismiss an enormously complex legal process in so bald a fashion? No matter how incurious the reader may be, his mind is flooded with a host of questions. Who else witnessed these star-chamber proceedings? Any disinterested zoophile or art connoisseur qualified to advise the justice? Any other gorillas? What assurance have we, indeed, that the exhibition took place in an atmosphere free of prejudice toward the lower order of primates? Lacking a court record or similar certified testimony, one is forced to reconstruct the circumstances as a paleontologist does a brontossaurus, from a single, ossified splinter. In my own restoration, which follows, none of the characters represent real persons, mid-Western or otherwise. The ape, however, is modelled after Ngonga, a young Lowlands gorilla with whom I conducted a half-hearted love affair last summer at the San Diego Zoo. And to her, in memory of what might have been, I dedicate it.

SCENE: *The private chambers of Milo Usufruct, a justice of the peace. A cheerless room dominated by a rolltop desk overflowing with writs, torts, and estoppels. A Globe-Wernicke sectional bookcase at left contains half a dozen moldy law books and a greenish pair of arctics. On the walls, two steel engravings, one of Blackstone and the other of a stag beleaguered by wolves. At rise, Usufruct is bent over a venerable, table-type Victor talking machine, fiddling at it with a screwdriver. He is a thin, bald radish of a man with watery, protuberant eyes. Miss Ripperger, his secretary and a woman polarized to attract every catastrophe, is unwrapping several phonograph records.*

USUFRUCT (*peevishly*): Something's scraping inside. There was nothing wrong with it when I put it away thirty years ago.

MISS RIPPERGER: It's probably all corroded. Or else somebody dropped it and smashed the mechanism.

USUFRUCT: If the mechanism was smashed, the turntable wouldn't revolve.

MISS RIPPERGER: You better not fool with that thing. You're liable to cut your finger and get blood poisoning. A nephew of mine—

A Girl and a Boy Anthropoid Were Dancing

USUFRUCT: Yes, yes. How about the records I wanted?

MISS RIPPERGER: They don't have any African tom-tom numbers.

USUFRUCT: Well, then, did you ask for wrestling music, like I told you?

MISS RIPPERGER: He said he never heard of any special songs a person could wrestle to. He gave me some Sousa marches—here's "Under the Double Eagle"—

USUFRUCT: Never mind, they'll do. That's all for now.

MISS RIPPERGER: If you'd give me more of an idea what it was for, I could try one of the big record stores downtown.

USUFRUCT: (*evasively*): Just a hearing I've called—doesn't matter. Now look, you go to lunch, and take an extra hour. I'm expecting a party, a Miss LaFlange.

MISS RIPPERGER: Is she the one in the Ziegler assault case?

USUFRUCT: Er—no, no, some theatrical mixup. Go on, run along. (*She exits. Her employer burrows into a desk drawer, produces a pocket mirror and comb, and trains a few filaments of hair across his scalp. He has seated himself and joined his fingertips judicially when a light knock sounds at the door. Opal LaFlange enters, carrying a fibre sample-case. She is a statuesque blonde clad in tomato-colored satin. A trifle steatopygous and endowed with what the poet Herrick has felicitously described as "that brave vibration each way free." Her flaxen hair, worn long over her shoulders, and milk-white skin recall to mind the pneumatic nudes who used to be portrayed on jackknives.*)

OPAL (*in a childish treble*): Hill-oo-oo! How are yoo-oo?

USUFRUCT: Ah, good morning! And how is our—ahem— little transgressor today?

OPAL: Just finely, judge. My, what a darling office! Is this where you do all your studying and stuff?

USUFRUCT: Yes, I—er—I'm a bug on privacy. You see, in my type work I have to get off by my lonesome and ponder over the—uh—briefs, so to speak, Do you like it?

OPAL: Oh, it's adorable! So snug and well—sort of anteem, if you know what I mean.

USUFRUCT: Precisely. No buttinskis around to distract —(*He starts as Opal zips open her dress and begins pulling it over her head.*) Hey, what are you doing there?

OPAL: Why, getting ready for my routine with Bombo. I thought you wanted to see the way we work in the clubs.

USUFRUCT (*scuttling to the door and shooting the bolt*): Sure, but after all, people might misunderstand. A man in my position can't be too careful.

OPAL: You can say that again, brother. (*She discards her slip.*) If anyone broke down that door right now, you'd have a hell of a time explaining.

USUFRUCT: L-listen, maybe we ought to skip it for the time being. I—I've got to run over to the Board of Estimate. I'll see your act at the Tropics tonight.

OPAL: Not unless you're a mind reader you won't. The coppers padlocked the joint three days ago.

USUFRUCT: Then we'll put it on in a field somewhere— at the Elks Club-house—

OPAL: Gorgeous, when I strip down to dance, I dance. Here, help me blow up Bombo. (*She draws an inert bundle of fur and a bicycle pump from the sample case, hands him the pump.*) This lousy valve in his belly button, it never did work right. . . . There. Now come on, lover, put your back into it.

USUFRUCT (*panting*): I . . . I'm doing the best I can . . . phew . . .

OPAL: Keep at it—the chest has to come out a whole foot yet. (*She spots the phonograph.*) Say, don't tell me! Got any fast tempo tunes—"Cow-Cow Boogie" or anything like that?

USUFRUCT (*the veins in his forehead bulging*): Uh . . . just those there. . . . Look, I'm getting winded. . . .

OPAL: "The Stars and Stripes Forever." "Semper Fidelis." "Washington Post March." Jeez, what cornball picked these out? (*The gorilla, a remarkable simulacrum with bared fangs, towers menacingly over Usufruct, who instinctively cowers away from it. A resounding blare of brass issues from the phonograph.*)

USUFRUCT: Good grief, are you crazy? Turn that noise down—we'll have the whole building in here!

OPAL: O.K., O.K., keep your girdle on. (*She mutes the music, detaches the pump, and twines the gorilla's arms about her.*) Well, here we go. Opening announcement, green dimmers on the lights, and we're on. (*She and Bombo rock across the floor, pantomiming a struggle to capsize each other. Suddenly, as Usufruct stares open-mouthed, a sharp knocking at the door is heard.*)

USUFRUCT: (*aghast*): Oh, my God. . . . Turn it off—*stop!*

OPAL: I can't—he's crushing me in his mighty arms—spare me, Bombo—

USUFRUCT (*babbling to himself*): I'm locked in here

with a mental case. (*He snaps off the phonograph, and with a strength born of desperation, wrenches apart Opal and Bombo.*)

OPAL: Take your hands off me, you popeyed little shrimp!

USUFRUCT: Sh-h-h! Get in the closet there, quick—your petticoat—no, no, don't put it on—wait a minute, the satchel too—(*As he thrusts her through the door and slams it, the knocking grows more insistent. In an agony of apprehension, he steals to the door and opens it. Flitcraft, the town's leading banker, and Zeugma, a retired merchant and pillar of the church, appear on the threshold. They exhibit obvious concern.*)

FLITCRAFT: Are you all right, Milo? We heard some sort of struggle—a crash—

ZEUGMA: We were afraid you had a seizure—apoplexy or something—

USUFRUCT (*with a ghastly attempt at jauntiness*): Who, me? Ah ha ha ha. . . .

ZEUGMA: Well, you do look kind of shaky, doesn't he, Simeon? Look at the cold sweat on his forehead.

USUFRUCT: I—I was trying to repair the ape—I mean, the apparatus—that is, the Victrola there. (*Sponging his brow*) Gentlemen, if you could come back in an hour—

FLITCRAFT (*entering*): Tell the truth, Milo, this is rather important; we'd like to have a little chin with you right now.

ZEUGMA: Yes, indeed. (*Grimly*) There are some very, very peculiar things going on in Tigris County, my friend. The sooner we put them right, the better. (*Usufruct twitches uncontrollably as his callers dispose themselves in chairs.*)

FLITCRAFT: Let's not beat around the bush, Milo. The political administration in this town is rotten to the core. You know who runs it? A lot of crooked gamblers, racketeers, and gorillas. (*Usufruct reacts, dislodges a phonograph record which shatters on the floor.*) My word, man, you're nervous today. What's wrong?

ZEUGMA: Shouldn't wonder he's coming down with the grippe.

FLITCRAFT: Yes, plenty of it around. Well, anyway, speaking for the law-abiding element in the community, Zeugma and I say they've made a monkey of us long enough.

USUFRUCT (*faintly*): Fellows, I feel a bit feverish. I—I believe I'll go on home and lie down for a spell.

FLITCRAFT: A very good idea, but first, tell me—have you ever thought of running for public office?

ZEUGMA: We need a decent, upright citizen to clean house. Throw the rascals out, that's my motto.

FLITCRAFT: Just so. Now, Milo, we've been over your record and your life is an open book. (*He breaks off, his eyes pinned on the closet door.*) Say, that's funny. What's that hanging out of there?

USUFRUCT (*teeth chattering*): A fur rug—a lap robe. You know, to cover up when you're driving in a sleigh. It b-belonged to my grandfather.

FLITCRAFT: Hmm. (*Rising*) If you don't mind, I'd like to see the rest of that robe. (*As he starts toward it, Usufruct frantically interposes himself.*)

USUFRUCT: Simeon, you've known me thirty years! I swear on everything holy that I never—

MISS RIPPERGER (*entering*): Mr. Flitcraft! Mr. Flitcraft!

FLITCRAFT: What is it?

MISS RIPPERGER: They just held up the bank—three men in a Buick coop! The police are chasing them down Wentworth Avenue!

FLITCRAFT: Great Scott! (*He runs out, followed by Zeugma. As they exit, Usufruct's knees buckle and he goes horizontal. Miss Ripperger hurries to him, and kneeling, begins to chafe his wrists.*)

MISS RIPPERGER: Oh . . . Oh . . . I just knew something was going to happen when I got up this morning! (*She raises her eyes inquiringly as the closet door opens.*)

CURTAIN

Duck, for the Night
Is Coming

Who, seeing me of a summer afternoon in the fashionable crush at the Plaza Auction Galleries, in a Savile Row suit and yellow dogskin gloves, my chin resting meditatively on a Malacca stick and acquiring some trifle of *boiserie*— my chin often acquires some trifle of *boiserie* independently of me—who, I repeat, would ever think of me as a connoisseur of livestock feed? Nobody would believe these tapering ivory fingers, from which elegantly depends a scented Egyptian cigarette, capable of detecting the sawdust that lurks in laying mash or distinguishing one oat from another, and, as a matter of fact, they're not. All I know about feeds is what I've just gleaned from an arresting piece in *Printers' Ink,* written by John L. Richardson, director of advertising and sales promotion for Allied Mills, Inc. Mr. Richardson's outfit, I learn, is no pipsqueak rural gristmill; it boasts upward of two hundred salesmen, serving four thousand dealers in thirty-two states, and it has evolved a means of stimulating their initiative so baroque that it warrants a short pause for stupefaction. "Try This Bikini on Your Salesmen," as the feuilleton is called, describes the method thus:

> Our problem at sales meeting time this year was to put over a new slogan, More Power to Ya!—and to do it with a bang. We let the meeting start out in the usual, dignified, slow-moving way. And then—Bing—bang—bop! The speaker pressed a carefully concealed contact button that caused an explosion through the top of some unassuming feed bags arranged nearby. A special combination of flash powder produced a miniature Bikini. But the explosions were not over. At this particular moment, sales portfolios entitled *More Power to Ya!—in 1951* were handed out with strict instructions not to open until all had been received so we could read all the contents together. The suspense was too great, of course, and first one and then another of the salesmen started to open them. A loaded cap device inside the front cover would explode, and a series of bangs would echo from various parts of the room. The presentation really went over.
>
> Each salesman was provided with extra caps for reloading before each presentation to dealers. Salesmen even tried them out at home on the wife and kids before presentation to dealers—something we had never before been able to do, no matter what we said about the value of practice sessions at home.

There is more here, *verständlich*, than meets the eye. In attempting to rouse its sales staff from lethargy, Allied

Mills has unwittingly illuminated the whole field of domestic relations, much as Perkin stumbled on aniline while
trying to synthesize quinine, or Captain Cook the Sandwich Islands in his quest of a new continent. But big business, avid for pounds and pence, has no time to waste on
sentiment; instead of recounting what took place when
the explosives were introduced into the family circle, the
article veers into a chesty recital of the accruing profits.
Rather than leave the reader tangled in a skein of hypothesis, I offer, in easily digestible narrative, one rationale
of the facts at hand. Unnecessary to add, anyone valorous
enough to venture into his neighborhood feed dealer's
hereafter may find it prudent to wear a crash helmet, not
to mention carry a Geiger counter.

PERSIS WYNKOOP lifted her eyes from the homemaking
magazine in which she had been studying, with some
perplexity, a recipe for nourishing an entire household on
a can of tuna, and listened intently. A car had turned in
to the driveway, mashing the hydrangea bush at the corner
of the porch. When, a few moments afterward, she heard
the apocalyptic crash of the garage door, her premonition
was confirmed; her liege had tarried on the way home
for a snifter with the boys. He generally used this playful
designation to describe the ritual, though sometimes, in
a surge of eloquence, he referred to it as a small libation
on the altar of friendship. Whatever the term, the result
was the same; Wally would materialize under full canvas,

like the *Flying Cloud*, his face aglow and his heart buoyed up to conquer any obstacle. In such moods, he was wont to consider himself irresistible—courtly as Sir Roger de Coverley, as gifted at repartee as Wilde, and a dancer to eclipse Vernon Castle. The phase Persis dreaded most, however, was his morning disillusion, the abysmal gloom and the forecasts of penury facing the Wynkoops. He would draw analogies to his career from "Death of a Salesman," plunge the breakfast table into despair, hector the children, and vanish, snug in the realization that he had disrupted everybody's day. Persis sighed. Maybe it was only exuberance caused by the annual sales meeting, or—she knew it was self-delusion—an unexpected raise. A single look at his face, radiant with bourbon, told her that the pattern was standard.

"Hi ya, honey!" There was no hint of unsteadiness in Wally's bearing or his bulky frame; he merely exuded a vast competence, an energy that made the room seem cramped. "You didn't wait dinner for me, did you?"

"No, I thought you'd be late," his wife said. "I'll fix you something—"

"Uh-uh, I had a bite on the train." He tossed his briefcase onto the couch, and as he turned back toward her, Persis noticed for the first time his singed eyebrow and the smudge on his cheek.

"You've been in a fight," she said automatically. "You've been rolling around in a bar."

"Who, me?" Pained innocence shone from his bloodshot eyes. "What are you talking about?"

"Your collar's scorched," Persis said. "What happened?"

"Nothing, I tell you," he said with a touch of asperity. "They pulled a kind of a gimmick at the sales meeting. Where're the kids?"

"Doreen's getting dressed to go out. Ben's in the cellar with his rocket."

Her husband chuckled sentimentally. "Boys never change," he said. "That kid'll get to the moon yet, damned if he won't. I ever tell you about the time I built a sloop in our cellar?"

"Yes, you did," admitted Persis.

"But you don't remember the pay-off," Wally said inexorably. "It was too big to get through the door. They still tell the story in Sheboygan."

"What story?" inquired Persis.

"About the sloop," he snapped. "Say, you must be in a fog or something." Rusty, the Wynkoop's elderly Airedale, had emerged meanwhile from the dinette, where he slept, and approached the couch. He gave Wally's briefcase a routine sniff, then backed away suddenly with a menacing growl.

"What is it, Rusty?" asked Persis, concerned. "I think he's scared." With an alacrity the matter hardly warranted, Wally caught up the briefcase and stowed it in a bookshelf. Persis watched him curiously. "What have you got in there, a gun?"

"Don't be silly," said her husband. His eyes shifted away from hers. "It's some papers—the new sales portfolio they gave us. Dog's getting punchy." The entrance of Doreen, booted and spurred for her date, rescued him from his wife's skeptical stare. Doreen, a pale, attenuated creature whose fancied resemblance to a *Vogue* model caused her to affect flower-like gestures and a marked hauteur, had dressed with some care. She had chosen a blouse and skirt of two clashing shades of green, blue platform shoes, and a scarlet cashmere stole. Her wrists and throat were festooned with an impressive assortment of charms and junk jewelry that tinkled and murmured like a gamelan orchestra as she moved.

"Daddy, dear." There was a note of gracious surprise in her greeting, as though she had encountered him in the Virgin Islands out of season. If her father's battered appearance startled her, she gave no sign.

Wally clucked appreciatively. "Hotsy-totsy. Pretty sharp. Who's your date, sweetness?"

"Paul Latham," replied Doreen, settling down on a hassock in a creditable imitation of Pavlova's Dying Swan.

"That drip?" Wally said with elaborate scorn. "He's dead on his feet."

"Will you keep quiet?" said Persis. "Doreen's old enough to pick her own beaux. And, what's more, try to be civil to him when he comes."

The injunction was well timed; a dragging footstep sounded on the porch, chimes jangled briefly, and Paul appeared, a faceless young man in a playtime jacket with two-tone lapels. After a feeble display of concern for the Wynkoops' health, he lapsed into a catatonic silence.

"Have a cigar," offered Wally abruptly, extracting two from his vest. Paul explained that smoking aggravated his sinuses, a statement Wally received with a grunt that unmistakably classified the youth as a pantywaist. At last, scratching around in desperation for a topic, Paul asked how the feed business was faring.

"Better than average," said Wally pridefully. "We're introducing a new leader into the line, Volcano Chick Ration."

"Now, Daddy, Paul doesn't want to hear that corny sales talk of yours," Doreen said, rising. Her father brushed aside the remark as unworthy of reply and reached down his briefcase from the shelf. "Like to see our new presentation?" he asked, in a tone that defied Paul to refuse. He drew forth a lavish portfolio whose cover, in four colors, portrayed a galaxy of prize calves, hogs, turkeys, and hens grouped around the emblem "Volcano Feeds—The Hallmark of Pep." "The idea of this is to dramatize our slogan to the dealers," he said. "Just take a gander inside."

Paul obeyed. There was a blinding flash and a whiplike report, and as Persis and Doreen screamed, a cloud of acrid smoke billowed upward from the title page. With a bound rivalling that of a Thomson's gazelle, Paul breasted the couch and went to earth behind it; simultaneously, a Niagara Falls souvenir plate balanced on top of a whatnot crashed to the floor. Rusty, his suspicions realized, fled yelping into the dinette.

The head of the house chortled. "How's that for an attention-getter, eh?" he crowed. "Come on out, Paul—the danger's over!"

The latter reappeared sheepishly, in apple-pie order save for a charred necktie. Doreen glared at her father for an instant, opened her mouth as though to speak, then forbore. Gathering up her cavalier, still somewhat dazed by his experience, she stalked out, her charms and bracelets quivering with indignation.

Persis, lips compressed, picked up a newspaper and began dispersing the remnants of smoke. "Well, I hope you're satisfied," she said, struggling to contain her irritation. "It'll be a long time before that one comes around here again."

"Oh, for God's sake!" exclaimed Wally. "Nag, nag, nag —nothing I do is right. What's so terrible? I was only testing out the portfolio to see how it would work on my prospects."

"Listen, Mr. Demolition," said his wife. "Your daughter's twenty-six years old and you might think of *her* prospects, too. You don't endear yourself to the boys by blowing them up the minute they walk in."

"Yeah? Well, if you're so desperate for a son-in-law that a mope like Paul Latham is the best—"

"Sh-h-h!" Persis cut in. The door chimes were sounding the strains of "Heilige Nacht." "Someone's coming. See who it is."

WALLY WENT OUT; a moment later, he returned, ushering in Vida and Fletcher Moultrie, the Wynkoops' next-door neighbors. Vida was avian, a dark, animated little woman whose quick eye missed nothing; her spouse, an accountant for a minor shipping firm and a genius at inducing tedium, had a bulbous head, like an onion, to which a pipe apparently had been welded at some remote date.

"There's nothing good on the television tonight," said Vida, in explanation of their presence, "so we thought we'd stop in and chin for a while." She sniffed suspiciously. "There's a funny smell in here, like gunpowder."

"Is there?" said Persis. "I hadn't noticed. Get some ice, Wally; the Scotch is in that end cupboard."

"None for me, thank you," said Moultrie.

"Nor me," said his wife, "but if you and Wally want to drink, don't mind us." Her tone clearly implied that scenes reminiscent of Hogarth's "Gin Lane" were enacted nightly *chez* Wynkoop. "Who was that with Doreen just now?"

"Paul Latham, from the bank. Why?"

"He seemed perfectly furious about something," Vida reported. "When Fletch and I passed him, I heard him say that he ought to have blackened somebody's eye." Wally, who had exhumed the Scotch and was pouring himself a pony, muttered contemptuously. Vida gave him a searching glance, saw the singed eyebrow, and was about to make inquiries, but her husband already had the floor.

"I hear Ben's building a rocket to fly to the moon." He smiled indulgently. "Think he'll make it?"

"I do," said Wally, bristling.

"Care to make a little bet?"

"You're damn right I will," retorted Wally, stung by the other's patronizing manner. "I've got five bucks that says—"

"Oh, come off it, Wally," Persis interrupted. "Don't you see Fletcher's teasing you?"

141

"Yes, and I'll tell *him* something," Wally said hotly. "They laughed at Lindy, too, but he got there."

"Not to the moon, he didn't," said Moultrie with Olympian condescension. "The reason nobody'll ever get there is because you can't overcome the gravitational pull of the earth. Any child knows that."

"Look, pal," said Wally, stabbing his neighbor's chest with his forefinger. "For two thousand years, wise guys like you have been saying that this can't be done and that can't be done—"

Fearful that his acrimony might flare into mayhem at any moment, Vida brought her consummate sense of tact into play. "The whole thing's idiotic," she said crisply. "Fletcher, you should know better than to argue with a person when he's in this—" She retrieved herself nimbly. "I mean, naturally he's proud of Ben, and you would be, too. Tell me, Wally," she said, turning to him with bright intensity, "everything O.K. at the plant?"

"I can't kick," said her host. "We're running eighteen per cent over this time last year. They released the figures at the sales meeting today."

"I guess that means a bonus, no?" asked Moultrie, striving to heal their rift.

"I hope I hope," said Wally. His eyes lit up. "Say, I'd like to spring a new sales approach on you people." Persis stiffened. "It's a novelty presentation we're distributing to our dealers."

"Wally," his wife said tautly. "*Please.*"

"Now, honey, you stay out of this," Wally said. "The promotion department told us to hold practice sessions at home, didn't they?" He turned his back on the company and fumbled awkwardly in the portfolio.

Persis got up, overcome with apprehension. She retreated several steps toward the kitchen. "You're crazy," she said breathlessly. "You don't know what you're doing."

The Moultries, frozen with curiosity, sat enthralled. Wally swung around, extending the portfolio to them with a flourish. *"Hocus-pocus dominocus!"* he declaimed. "Presenting the greatest assortment of blue-ribbon feeds ever offered by Marvel Mills. Look 'em over, folks!"

Moultrie studied the cover, cocked his head critically, and nodded approval to Vida, craning over his shoulder. Then, with the same reverence he might have accorded the Book of Kells, he opened it.

When the smoke cleared sufficiently for Persis to again discern their faces, a substantial change had come over them. Fletcher Moultrie looked like one of Lew Dockstader's minstrels, though less amiable. The pipe had been wrenched out of his teeth and its coals smoldered in his clothing. Vida was mottled an unattractive gray and pink; the switch with which she supplemented her coiffure hung precariously from her crown, swaying gently in the afterblast. Turned to stone, Persis stood helpless before the wrath to come.

Wally threw back his head and guffawed. "Bull's-eye!" he shouted. "I knew you'd get a bang out of our campaign!"

Moultrie raised himself from his chair, walked to the fireplace with a peculiar, stiff-legged gait, and picked up the poker.

Suddenly a maniacal yell rang out from the basement, followed by the high-pitched voice of an adolescent boy. "Clear the runway!" it warned. "All lunar space craft beware! Contact!" An instant later, a weird projectile, straddled by a small figure, his head encased in a cylindrical helmet, ripped through the floor with explosive force at the point where Wally stood and disappeared through the ceiling, travelling at about four miles a minute. For almost ten seconds after it had passed, absolute silence hushed the room.

Then Persis spoke, in a tentative, almost wheedling tone. "Wally?" she said. "Where are you, Wally?" There was no reply. She shrugged and, warily circling the hole in the floor, uncorked the bottle of Scotch. "Well," she said with fatalistic calm, "that's that. How about a little snifter?"

Exit Pagliacci,
Beefing

Do you suppose I'd get anywhere if I made a timid suggestion to the New York *Times*, a publishing enterprise that has managed to keep its head above water for ninety-nine years without my suggestions? I have a wrinkle that may not have occurred to its directors, an all-purpose hunch guaranteed to swell their coffers, fatten the take-home dividends, and delight the readership, all at the outlay of not so much as a bent farthing, and I'd like to see the efficiency engineer who could score a comparable triple play. Nutshell-brief, the idea is this. At present, the *Times* appears in four different forms: There is the ordinary newsstand, or bloodcurdler, edition; the international edition, for overseas subscribers; the microfilm edition; and the permanent, rag-paper version, beamed at libraries and cornerstones. What I contemplate is a fifth form, of a volatile nature, which would disappear instantly upon being read and thus hamstring children from using it to humiliate their parents. It might even be printed on some edible substance like tortillas or Swedish health bread, so you could swallow the pages as you finished them. I'll leave flavor and physical details to the composing room; my only interest is in checkmating juvenile initiative at the source. If I can just prevent items like "Proud Father" from falling into the hands of my young and kindling their imagination, the sceptre is mine again. In other words, God and Sulzberger willing, the *Times* will be slightly invisible to adolescents; there'll be no petards, and nobody hoist.

"Proud Father" was a dispatch contained in the *Times* Sunday movie section and was concerned with an acute case of paternal love that had stricken a wealthy sawmill operator named Dan Gunn, Jr. This worthy, the report stated, "came up to Hollywood from his home town, Woodville, Texas . . . to see about putting his 9-year-old daughter Judy on the screen. But," the dispatch continued, "Gunn had no ambitions to make her a film star. All he wanted was to get her into a picture so that people—'lots and lots of people'—could hear her play the piano. Moreover, he had no foolish notions about convincing some producer that he ought to risk his own money on such a project, arriving fully prepared to spend his own dollars for the purpose. So last week, as Papa Gunn looked on proudly and producer-director Wes Beeman had everything in order, the first scenes of a two-reel musical short in Ansco color entitled 'Fantasy for Judy' went before the cameras at the Eagle-Lion studio. As a showcase for the little pianist, it will bring her to the screen playing three numbers, Mozart's 'Turkish March,' Grieg's 'Nocturne,' and Chopin's 'Ecossais,' while a troupe of ballet dancers directed by Michael Panaieff enlivens the scene in pantomime. This little venture into the world of the cinema will cost Judy's father between $25,000 and $30,000. 'But shucks,' he said, 'if it does what I want it to do, that will be cheap. Definitely,' he added, 'I'm not raising no movie star. This is a case of genius—musical genius—coming out in a 9-year-old child, and I just can't hoard it. But I'm glad I got money enough so that no one else can own so much as one of her fingernails.'"

Snatching at an opportunity to draw a vivid moral lesson, I clipped the story, scrawled a disdainful "Fulsome" in the margin, and left it on my twelve-year-old daughter's vanity, together with a bag of sweets. There, I reflected, this will demonstrate that one needn't spend thirty grand on a valentine to prove his fatherly affection. Faugh on parvenus who subsidize their children's love with bread and circuses. I made no further reference to my magnanimity other than to mention it to my wife and intimate several times to the child that the confections had cost ten cents, throwing in a homily decrying the folly of parvenus who subsidize their children's love. I can conscientiously say that up to that juncture I was boss man of the family and big wheel, and that no domestic sparrow fell without my cognizance.

OVER THE NEXT couple of months, though, I began detecting a chain of suspicious eddies in the smooth current of our household life. A strange acquisitiveness suddenly possessed my daughter and her fourteen-year-old brother. They demanded increased allowances, liquidated for a sizable quantity of cash the stamp collections they had amassed, economized on their lunches, and banked every penny. They had both been earning substantial salaries from part-time work, soldering cheap jewelry after school hours in a closet I had fitted up for them with a real electric bulb. To my chagrin, I discovered they were diverting the money, which had permitted me Havana cigars, massages, and other small luxuries I could not otherwise have afforded, into their own savings account. I remonstrated with them, denouncing such avarice as indicative of a contemptible meanness of spirit, but they countered with double-talk and evasive fleers. Undoubtedly they were emboldened by my temperate approach, for they now spread their wings. Taking advantage of the reputation for probity I had built up across the years in rural Pennsylvania, they secretly negotiated a second mortgage on our farm—a chilling instance of the guile youngsters conceal under a cloak of innocence. Just as they were about to pawn my studs at Simpson's, my patience evaporated and I lowered the boom on them.

"What in Tophet's going on around here?" I shouted. "You little devils are cooking up some mischief, and, by the Eternal, I'll root it out if it's the last—"

I stopped short as my son withdrew a letter from his jumper and extended it to me. "This just came for you," he said. "We were going to surprise you after dinner, when you're logy, but you're bound to know anyhow."

Blinking, I unfolded and read the note. It was a blunt, matter-of-fact message from Iris Productions, Inc., a documentary-film group with studios located on Tenth Avenue. Shooting on "Fantasy for Sidney," the one-reel novelty featuring my chalk-talk specialty, would commence the following morning at nine, and I was instructed to report in full makeup on the set with my easel, smock, and a change of Windsor ties.

"Good grief, I'm no movie actor!" I sputtered, overwhelmed. "Why, I haven't given a chalk talk since the Older Business Boys' Get-Together at the Providence Y in 1919!"

"No, but you've been gassing about it ever since," said my wife, a woman afflicted with total recall. "Two drinks and you start browbeating our friends with that stale patter of yours. The evenings I've spent—"

"One moment, Mrs. James Gibbons Huneker," I said crushingly. "If I'd wanted to exploit my talent, I could have had my name in lights."

"And you still will, Daddy," chimed in my son loyally. "This is a case of genius—artistic genius—coming out in a forty-six-year-old man, and we just can't hoard it. Promoting the geetus for your celluloid bow has tested us tads to the utmost, but we deem it measly for a progenitor which he's gifted beyond mortal ken."

Hot salt tears welled up at the spontaneous tribute that had sprung from a candid heart, and I resolved on the instant to vindicate his faith. Long after the family had retired that night, I paced the floor composing graceful sallies to refurbish my routine, cultivating the ironical raised eyebrow that had boosted Jan Kiepura to fame, and practicing deep, pear-shaped tones. Silly as I knew it to be, there nevertheless kept recurring in my mind's eye a vignette of myself in a vicuña coat, piloting a sleek yellow Jaguar into Romanoff's amid envious whispers. I didn't know how I was going to get it through the front door, but I felt certain Mike would have a table ready for the town's foremost Thespian. I envisioned myself dancing with taffy-haired starlets at the Mocambo, trading punches with Humphrey Bogart at Chasen's over some trifling insult, responding to toasts at Academy dinners. Come hell or high water, I determined to raise a hairline mustache.

"THEATRICAL HISTORY" is not a phrase to bandy about, but I know no other to describe what I made the next forenoon at the Iris studio. Mustard-keen and as poised as Lowell Sherman, I showed I was that rare player who can surmount a disastrous head cold, a jealous director,

and bungling technicians, and deliver a virtuoso performance. After a slow start, due to straying into a production
that dealt with cross-fecundation, I quickly picked up mo-
mentum. With lightning strokes, I limned a hundred
amusing conceits: a profile of William Jennings Bryan,
his hair curled into a bird's nest full of eggs; a bag of
money that transposed astonishingly into a silk-hatted
capitalist; a simple hieroglyph of a bayonet and a canine
tail that represented a soldier leading a dog past a fence.
This repertoire, deftly interthreaded with witticisms that
ran like quicksilver, tickled every funny bone; even the
electricians, inured to the antics of professional comedians, unashamedly held their sides. In stealing the spotlight from the director, naturally, I incurred his undying
enmity. He cunningly tried to inveigle me into accepting
a Hawaiian singing ensemble in the background, on the
plea that the audience would welcome intervals of musical
relief, and, when rebuffed, proposed to cut in flashes of
Smith & Dale, the old Palace favorites, belaboring each
other with pig bladders. The poor chap did not realize
that you do not enhance the beauty of the Venus de Milo
by setting a clock in her stomach. Philistine that he was,
he doubtless had never seen sheer perfection before, and
it blinded him.

"When d'ye think the thing'll be ready to preview?"
I asked him carelessly as the cameras quit grinding. "I'd
like to ask a few friends." He made some inarticulate
remark about giving them corrosive sublimate instead
and stalked off. I saw at once that my screen career hung
on a wisp of gossamer, and might well end on the

cutting-room floor. Yet when I got home I gave no hint of disquiet to the children, who were waiting eagerly. Their faces glowed with anticipation at the thought of my film début; I knew that in their naïve pantheon I already outshone even such gods as Red Skelton and Donald O'Connor.

PERHAPS THE TRYOUT of the picture would have been more auspicious had I not intrusted it to my offspring but instead arranged it in person. It was unveiled at an owl show in a Forty-second Street flea bag, complementing an Italian sex thriller called "Vesuvio," in which Anna Magnani kept erupting from her shirtwaist, and "Cuties in Bondage," a sociological study of Hollywood high-school girls shanghaied into white slavery. An audience of sailors and dice hustlers, while visibly impressed, received it quietly, according me the respect of muting their laughs so that my every syllable emerged distinctly. Indeed, at times I seemed almost *too* audible; whenever I cleared my throat, a reedy noise like a musical saw issued from the sound track, inspiring a gang of toughs in the balcony to reply with catcalls. The reactions of our guests, two couples we had entertained at a small dinner party prior to the showing, were of necessity fragmentary, since they had to leave in the middle to judge some beagles at Fishers Island. The children, who had been allowed to stay up late as a special treat befitting producers, gave the short an unhesitating accolade. They

stamped their feet and applauded wildly, alerting everyone around them to the presence of the star and the fact
that he was available for autographs. Peacockery of that
sort, however, has always been distasteful to me, and I
arose, muffling my face in my coat collar. The whole
family, with the exception of my wife, besought me to
remain for the vulture show, at 2:30 A.M., but Sardi's
called to the actor's blood in my veins, and the summons
could not be ignored.

Nothing is ever left undone to stifle a masterpiece, and
one day posterity will agree that "Fantasy for Sidney"
shared the usual fate. The jackals of the press, aware that
it presaged a revolution in the flicker industry, united in
a ruthless campaign of silence. Finally, one exhibitor
more courageous than his fellows released it in his art
cinema below Fourteenth Street, in concert with two ex-
perimental subjects depicting a Meccano set interpreting
a Sibelius symphony and Jean Cocteau shaving his right
eyeball. "Morpheus Rides Again," as the package was
styled, opened of a Friday night. By Saturday morning,
six pickets from the Children's Aid Society were patrolling
the sidewalk. They flaunted placards condemning para-
sites who use child labor to forward their careers, and
urged a boycott and a police investigation. Midway
through my sequence in the evening performance, a bomb
planted by some fanatic exploded, but as there was nobody in the theatre at the time, the damage was relatively
minor. On Sunday, the management announced the return of "The Cabinet of Dr. Caligari" by popular demand,

and the Wizard of the Chalk Talk was as extinct as the passenger pigeon.

Since then, I've rather lost touch with pictures and, in fact, with my children. I understand they're out on the Coast currently, trying to interest a Texan (a sawmill tycoon, I believe) in producing "Sappho," with his nine-year-old daughter in the part created by Olga Nethersole. They'll probably want me for a character bit, but, frankly, it's not my medium. I'll take an armchair at the Lambs, a tin of Velvet Joe, and the ephemeral edition of the New York *Times*. All the rest, for my dough, is illusion.

Watch the Birdie
and Shield the Beezer

Once upon a time (in fact, about six months ago), there was a vast, potent combine of whiskey distillers named Schenley, with untold gallons of barrelled sunlight in its warehouses, which set out to win my patronage. In me, the combine felt, it had a Homeric bibber who could empty those warehouses if he was cozened sweetly enough. To this end, Schenley instituted a particularly intense advertising campaign, featuring noted stars of stage and screen who extolled its tipple as the passport to an enchanted evening. For months, every time I opened a newspaper or magazine, some luminary like Ezio Pinza would dimple out at me over a highball glass, beseeching me to try that smoother, more sociable blend.

155

The Ill-Tempered Clavichord

After limitless wood pulp had been expended in a barren attempt to dispel my apathy—I went right on doggedly drinking New Jersey applejack—the attack shifted to the billboards. Ruddy with good-fellowship and Schenley, the faces of Hollywood's favorite sons bloomed in four colors along each byway I traversed; romantic leads, comedians, and character actors alike beamed endorsement of the magic brand. The outdoor phase reached its apogee in a gigantic painting of Cesar Romero I saw just before Thanksgiving at the Manhattan end of the Holland Tunnel. Even life-size, Romero's face had always seemed to me the epitome of Latin menace; enlarged forty times it was a spectacle to freeze the hand to the steering wheel. I drove helterskelter through the tunnel, knees trembling, and pulled up at the first available tavern in Jersey City for a quick jolt. Unluckily, in my agitation I forgot the name of the whiskey Romero was sponsoring, and gulped down whatever was put before me, with the result that my evening was measurably less enchanted than it might have been.

Apparently, Schenley decided from reports furnished by its far-flung secret service that it was getting nowhere with me, because a couple of weeks later it flexed its corporate thews and made a really desperate bid to arrest my attention. There appeared in the metropolitan journals a six-column pre-holiday advertisement captioned "We're all giving Schenley . . . why don't you? Join these stars who drink and serve Schenley." The stars, clad in formal evening wear and grasping upraised glasses, were Louis Hayward, Herbert Marshall, Robert Preston, Claude

Rains, and Cesar Romero. They were clustered around a buffet table laden with a baked ham, the symbolism of which was not especially felicitous, and they registered every degree of gratification from subdued smirk to ravished delight. The accompanying letterpress embroidered the theme that since screen stars can be trusted to choose the best (an assumption the copy writer might have a sticky time defending), the average citizen should lose no time in guzzling that smoother, more sociable et cetera.

Unshaken by this transparent effort to overwhelm me with sheer numbers, I was turning the page when a curious suspicion seized me. Influential though Schenley was, how had it persuaded five celebrated actors to pose harmoniously in the same photograph, their only bond the one the whiskey was bottled in? It must have required the tact of a Disraeli to soothe their professional vanities, to assure each that he would be displayed to advantage, to jockey the quintet into wholesale camaraderie. I took another and closer peek at the picture, and in a flash the whole thing stood revealed. None of the actors' heads seemed actually to fit the bodies below; apparently they had been snipped out sketchily from other shots and superimposed on the trunks of persons unknown in evening dress.

One fact was inescapable, however: Five men in full-dress suits had posed for the convivial scene and altruistically sacrificed their features in the struggle to break down my sales resistance. What satanic pressures had induced them to comply? What turbulent emotions had

157

stirred them during the process? The more I speculate about these anonymous victims of commerce, the more obsessed I become with them. Partly to rid myself of the obsession and partly to adumbrate the plight of five fellow-mortals snared in such a peculiar web, I submit a conjectural playback of what took place in the photographer's studio. Needless to say, if it turns out that the visages of the stars were merely pasted on tailor's dummies, my whole beautiful hypothesis falls like a house of cards.

SCENE: *The studio of Egmont Shillito, a prominent commercial photographer. As the curtain rises, Brabant and Cortelyou, two young male models, are revealed posed in extremely wooden, rigid attitudes on a dais sprinkled with cotton. They are clad in cable-stitch sweaters and mittens; Brabant is addressing a golf ball with a niblick, and Cortelyou is poising a tennis racket for an overhead smash. Suddenly the black cloth that drapes the camera trained on them is flung aside, and Shillito, a snappish hyperthyroid, pops out.*

SHILLITO: (*reedily*): No! No! It's impossible! You haven't caught the mood at all! You're too animated! You look like normal human beings!

BRABANT: Gee whizz, Mr. Shillito, we're deadpanning it the best we can.

SHILLITO (*supplicating*): Listen, boys, can't I hammer it through your skull? We're doing this for a *knitting* manual. You've got to be as expressionless as a doll. One speck of feeling and you destroy the impact of the knit goods!

CORTELYOU: Mr. Shillito, do you mind if I make a suggestion?

SHILLITO: What?

CORTELYOU: These athaletic accessories don't go with the background. Wouldn't it be more realistic if we had snowshoes or a Flexible Flyer?

SHILLITO: (*savagely*): Who wants realism, idiot? It's just the reverse I'm trying to get! Realism frightens those old bags that buy the wool! (*A tumult offstage, and Bracegirdle, a dominant, incisive advertising executive, enters in a swirl of camel's-hair coat.*)

BRACEGIRDLE: All right, Shillito, clear the decks. I've got those Schenley models parked outside.

SHILLITO: Do they look anything like the actors?

BRACEGIRDLE: Anything *like?* For God's sake, man, we've spent sixty thousand rutabagas combing the country for their exact doubles! Their own mothers wouldn't know them apart!

SHILLITO: Perfect. Bring 'em in. (*Handing Brabant and Cortelyou some stage currency*) Here, you guys, drink some ale and see a double feature. I want you really slugged when we shoot the scene this afternoon. (*As they nod and straggle out, five men in evening clothes—Breitigam, Twyeffort, Krebs, Marple, and Hackamore—straggle in. Since this complex bit of theatrical mechanics could easily demolish the set, it might be prudent to engage a director of the stature of Max Reinhardt, several of whom can always be found at Walgreen's in Times Square.*)

BRACEGIRDLE (*triumphantly*): Well, what do you think of them, Egmont? Some resemblance, what?

SHILLITO: Jiminy, I'll say. . . . Look here, are you sure those two on the end aren't Herbert Marshall and Claude Rains?

BRACEGIRDLE: I wasn't at first, but they showed me credentials proving that they're nonentities.

SHILLITO: They might have forged them.

BRACEGIRDLE: No, they also had distinctive strawberry marks. Our agency doctors examined Rains and Marshall, and they had no distinctive strawberry marks.

SHILLITO: O.K., then, we may as well get started. Group them around that refectory table, will you? Here's a plastic ham and a bowl of shredded paper, if you need salad or any props like that.

BRACEGIRDLE: Fine. Right this way, men. Now, just line up there with your shoulders touching and raise your drinks. That's the ticket. It's New Year's Eve and you're holding high wassail, see?

MARPLE: Ahem. I don't quite feel it, Mr. Bracegirdle.

BRACEGIRDLE: Feel what?

MARPLE: The scene. It's too static. Looking at it through the eyes of Cesar Romero, you might say, I don't sense any way to exploit his gifts.

BRACEGIRDLE: Yes, yes, I realize there's nothing to get your teeth into—

MARPLE (*eagerly*): But there could be. Why not have the other four laying around on a settee, sort of half crocked, while I'm tickling their risibilities with a funny routine?

BRACEGIRDLE: Do you envision them as facing the camera at all?

MARPLE: Well, candidly, no. The emphasis should be on the one personality the public knows—that is, Romero.

TWYEFFORT (*bristling*): I suppose nobody ever heard of Louis Hayward, eh? Did you see "The Fortunes of Captain Blood"?

MARPLE: No, I left after the feature. I didn't stay for the kapok.

BRACEGIRDLE: Here, stop that scrimmaging. We've got a job to do. This is a dress rehearsal, so pull together. Up glasses and project! (*As Hackamore flags him*) What is it, Mr. Rains— I mean Mr. Hackamore?

HACKAMORE: I beg pardon, but I think this Old-Fashioned I'm raising is a false note. Claude Rains drinks only Cuba Libres.

BRACEGIRDLE: Humph, very interesting. Are you Claude Rains?

HACKAMORE: No, of course not, but being as I'm practically his twin, I've made a close study of his tastes, and he would never—

BRACEGIRDLE: One moment. What's your full name?

HACKAMORE: Why, Florian J. Hackamore.

BRACEGIRDLE: Good. Well, I'll relieve your anxiety. This is a picture of Florian J. Hackamore holding high wassail with his friends.

HACKAMORE: Is that what it's going to say under the picture?

BRACEGIRDLE (*quivering*): Why?

HACKAMORE: Because in that event I'd have to be paid extra. It'd be like a kind of testimonial.

BRACEGIRDLE: Hackamore, in about two minutes you're going to find yourself shambling along Fifty-third Street in an acute state of unemployment. (*The other subsides.*) Now, remember, all of you, when Mr. Shillito says he's ready, give him the old reaction. Roll your eyes, smack your lips, punch home the festive holiday cheer that comes of a smoother—

KREBS: Mr. Bracegirdle, would you want me to suppress something if I knew it was going to spoil the ad?

BRACEGIRDLE: Certainly not. What's the trouble?

KREBS: Robert Preston's a mixer, a hail-fellow-well-met. He wouldn't hang on the outskirts of the bunch, the way I am. He'd be right in the middle, garnering all the laffs.

BRACEGIRDLE (*fuming*): I don't care a tinker's damn—

KREBS: Besides, it's not fair to stick him off on the edge. He's a lot bigger draw than these other crumbs.

BREITIGAM (*rounding on his colleague*): Oh, he is, is he? Look up *Variety's* box-office score on my last— I mean Marshall's last picture!

KREBS: I have. You stunk in Cleveland.

BREITIGAM: Step outside, you big tub of lard, and I'll show you whether Bart Marshall's washed up yet!

TWYEFFORT: In spades! Louis Hayward wouldn't overlook a crack like that and I won't either!

BRACEGIRDLE (*screaming*): Shillito! Shillito! Where are you?

SHILLITO (*reappearing from beneath his black tent*): Under here. Say, what's with these lugs? I don't capture any yuletide spirit on the plate.

BRACEGIRDLE: I want five paper bags and I want 'em fast! Don't ask any questions, just get 'em!

SHILLITO: Sure, right in this cabinet. (*Apologetically*) They're a little soiled; the delicatessen forgot to put waxed paper on the sandwiches.

BRACEGIRDLE (*grimly*): Doesn't matter. Pass 'em out, one to each man. . . . Check. Now, gentlemen, kindly put those on.

SHILLITO: He means like paper hats, boys. To heighten the party atmosphere.

BRACEGIRDLE: No, I don't. Right down over your phizes —way down. (*Rubbing his hands*) Capital, and here are your libations. All set for the take, Professor.

HACKAMORE (*muffled*): How you going to get our expression through these?

BRACEGIRDLE: Don't worry, we'll use a special X-ray lens. Well, Egmont, how does it strike you?

SHILLITO (*cocking his head*): A mighty effective shot. It leaves something to the imagination. Ought to sell a lot of liquor.

BRACEGIRDLE: Well, I don't know what the client will think, but *I* like it. And, of course, we can always play around later with the negative, if need be.

SHILLITO: I wouldn't touch it. After all, you can't improve on perfection.

BRACEGIRDLE: Hmm, very well phrased. (*Thoughtfully lighting a cigar*) I wonder whether we couldn't evolve that into a whiskey slogan?

CURTAIN

Rock-a-Bye, Viscount,
in the Treetop

☞

A COUPLE OF MONTHS BACK, the firm of Bramhall & Rixey, Ltd., a shipping concern on lower Broadway operating a string of freighters to West African ports, received an unusual communication. It was inscribed in pencil on both sides of a sheet of lined yellow paper of the sort commonly employed in secondary schools, and its numerous erasures and interlineations attested to the care that had gone into its composition. The correspondent identified himself as a prominent New York sportsman and big-game hunter who was contemplating a safari into the heart of the Dark Continent (Africa, he explained in a helpful aside). Without going into wearisome detail, he was in a position to assure Bramhall & Rixey that the expedition would eclipse anything of the kind on record. Not only was he planning to bring back a number of gorillas, man-eating lions, and comparably gaudy fauna but, if time allowed, he proposed to search out King Solomon's mines and corroborate the existence of a mysterious white goddess ruling a vast empire of blacks in the Cameroons. Obviously, any wide-awake shipping company could appreciate what enormous publicity must accrue to it if chosen to transport such an enterprise. Should Bramhall & Rixey agree to carry the party—without charge, of course— the sportsman thought he might prevail on his associates to assent, though he warned that they rather favored a rival fleet. Stressing the need for an immediate decision, due to the impending monsoon rains (whether in Manhattan or Africa he did not specify), the writer enclosed a self-addressed postal for a speedy reply.

My first reaction when I came across a postal in my morning mail several days ago with the terse admonition "Wipe your nose, bub," signed by Bramhall & Rixey, was one of spontaneous irritation. I caught up the phone, forgetting for the moment that my fourteen-year-old son had been enthralled this past summer by a book called "Tarzan of the Apes" and that he had been treating the family to a sustained panegyric on Africa. "I'll teach you whose nose to wipe!" I shouted into it. "I've half a mind to come down and cane you people publicly in Beaver Street!" Fortunately, they were spared the humiliation, as, in my wrath, I forgot to dial their number, and by the time I tumbled to the probable culprit and documented his guilt, I was able to take a much more lenient view of the incident. The fact of the matter is that back in 1918, the year I myself first encountered Edgar Rice Burroughs' electrifying fable, it exercised a similarly hypnotic effect on me. Insofar as the topography of Rhode Island and my physique permitted, I modelled myself so closely on Tarzan that I drove the community to the brink of collapse. I flung spears at the neighbors' laundry, exacerbated their watchdogs, swung around their piazzas gibbering and thumping my chest, made reply only in half-human grunts interspersed with unearthly howls, and took great pains generally to qualify as a stench in the civic nostril. The hallucination passed as abruptly as it had set in; one morning I awoke with an overwhelming ennui for everything related to Africa, weak but lucid. My kinsfolk were distrustful for a while, but as soon as they saw me constructing a catamaran in which to explore the Everglades, they knew I was rational again.

CURIOUS AS TO WHY Tarzan had enraptured two generations and begotten so many sequels, movie serials, and comics, I commandeered my son's copy of the novel and my wife's chaise longue and staged a reunion. Like most sentimental excursions into the past, it was faintly tinged with disillusion. Across the decades, Burroughs' erstwhile jaunty narrative had developed countless crow's-feet and wrinkles; passages that I remembered outracing Barney Oldfield now seemed to puff and wheeze like a donkey engine. The comparison was aided by a donkey engine puffing directly outside my window, and frequently, in all honesty, its rhythmic snoring was amplified by my own. Nevertheless, I got the gist of the story, and for gist-lovers who prefer to sniff the candy at long range, that little may suffice.

Strictly speaking, the saga begins in the African forest with the adoption by a female anthropoid ape of an English baby of lofty lineage, but to render this association feasible, if not palatable, some valiant exposition is required. Lord and Lady Greystoke, outward bound on the barkentine *Fuwalda* from Freetown in the summer of 1888, are en route "to make a peculiarly delicate investigation of conditions" in a British West Coast colony when mutiny breaks out among the crew. Considering that the captain and his mates are forever emptying revolvers into the men and felling them with belaying pins, Burroughs' appraisal of the situation is dazzlingly understated: "There was in the whole atmosphere of the craft that undefinable something which presages disaster." The lid ultimately blows off, and a lamentable scene ensues: "Both sides were cursing and swearing in a frightful manner, which, together with the reports of the firearms and the screams and groans of the wounded, turned the deck of the *Fuwalda* to the likeness of a madhouse." Lord Greystoke, however, behaves with the sang-froid one expects of a British peer; through it all, he "stood leaning carelessly beside the companionway puffing meditatively upon his pipe as though he had been but watching an indifferent cricket match." After the mutineers have disposed of authority, the fate of the couple trembles briefly in the balance. Then Black Michael, the ringleader, intercedes for them and persuades his colleagues to maroon the Greystokes in a secluded spot. The speech transmitting this decision somehow recalls the rhetoric of Gilbert and Sullivan's magnanimous scalawags. "You may be all right," he explains kindly, "but it would be a hard matter to land you in civilization without a lot o' questions being asked, and none o' us here has any very convincin' answers up our sleeves."

To skim over the rest of the prologue, the blue bloods survive the immediate rigors of life in the bush; Greystoke, exhibiting a virtuosity rarely met with in castaways and almost never in the House of Lords, builds a stuccoed log cabin furnished with cozy appurtenances like bamboo curtains and bookcases, and his wife, materially aiding the story line, presents him with a male child. But all unbeknownst to the patrician pair, their hourglass is already running out. Her Ladyship, badly frightened by a marauding ape, expires on the boy's first birthday, and as her husband sits stricken at the deathbed, a band of apes bent on stealing his rifle invade the cabin and kill him. Among them is Kala, a female whose own babe has just been destroyed by the king of the tribe. Obeying what Burroughs reverently terms "the call of universal motherhood within her wild breast," and the even greater urgency for a gimmick to set the narrative rolling, she snatches up the English tot, deposits her lifeless one in its cradle, and streaks into the greenery. The blueprint is now technically complete, but the author, ever a man to pile Pelion upon Ossa, contrives an extra, masterly touch. Since the cabin contains the schoolbooks from which the lad will learn to read eventually, as well as his father's diary—capriciously written in French—proving his identity, it must be preserved intact. The king ape, therefore, accidentally discharges Greystoke's gun and, fleeing in terror, slams the door shut. Burroughs may foozle his prose on occasion, but when it comes to mortising a plot, he is Foxy Grandpa himself.

It would serve no useful purpose to retrace the arduous youthhood and adolescence of Tarzan (whose name, incidentally, means "White-Skin," there being no equivalent for Greystoke in ape language), his sanguinary triumphs over a long roster of enemies like leopards, pythons, and boars, and his easy emergence as undisputed boss of the jungle. Superior heredity, of course, gives "the aristocratic scion of an old English house" a vast edge over his primitive associates. Thanks to the invaluable schoolbooks in the cabin, he instinctively learns to read and write—not without hardship, for, says Burroughs, "of the meaning and use of the articles and conjunctions, verbs and adverbs and pronouns, he had but the faintest and haziest conception." But he perseveres, and along with literacy come further civilized attributes. He bathes assiduously, covers his nakedness with pelts, and, out of some dim recess of his consciousness, produces a really definitive method of distinguishing himself from brute creation: "Almost daily, he whetted his keen knife and scraped and whittled at his young beard to eradicate this degrading

169

emblem of apehood. And so he learned to shave—rudely and painfully, it is true—but, nevertheless, effectively." No reasonably astute reader needs to be told twice that when the hero of a popular novel, whether he is Willie Baxter or an ape man, starts shaving, a pair of mischievous blue eyes are right around the corner. However astute, though, no reader could possibly anticipate a simp of the proportions of Jane Porter, or the quartet of frowzy vaudeville stereotypes that now bumbles into the picture.

The newcomers, it appears, are a party of treasure-seekers hailing from Baltimore, headed by an absent-minded pedagogue called Professor Archimedes Q. Porter, complete with frock coat and shiny plug hat. In his retinue are Samuel T. Philander, an elderly fusspot secretary straight from the pages of *Puck;* Esmeralda, a corpulent Negro maid aquiver with fear and malapropisms; his daughter Jane, whose beauty ravishes the senses; and, finally, Charley-horsing the long arm of coincidence, Tarzan's own cousin and the incumbent Lord Greystoke, William Cecil Clayton. They, too, have just been embroiled in a ship's mutiny—Burroughs' favorite literary calamity, evidently—and are now marooned in Tarzan's very parish. Using these piquant ingredients for all they are worth, the author hereupon proceeds to stir up the most delirious chowder of larceny, homicide, aboriginal passion, and haphazard skulduggery ever assembled outside the Newgate calendar. In all this, Tarzan plays the role of the Admirable Crichton, snatching each of the characters, in turn, from the jaws of death and, inevitably, turning Jane Porter's head. The section in which she betrays her partiality for him is a sockdolager. Tarzan is putting the kayo on Terkoz, a bull ape who has abducted Jane: "As the great muscles of the man's back and shoulders knotted beneath the tension of his efforts, and the huge biceps and forearm held at bay those mighty tusks, the veil of centuries of civilization and culture was swept from the blurred vision of the Baltimore girl. When the long knife drank deep a dozen times of Terkoz' heart's blood, and the great carcass rolled lifeless upon the ground, it was a primeval woman who sprang forward with outstretched arms toward the primeval man who had fought for her and won her. And Tarzan? He did what no red-blooded man needs lessons in doing. He took his woman in his arms and smothered her upturned, panting lips with kisses. For a moment Jane Porter lay there with half-closed eyes. . . . But as suddenly as the veil had been withdrawn it dropped again, and an outraged conscience suffused her face with its scarlet mantle, and a mortified woman thrust Tarzan of the Apes from her and buried her face in her hands. . . . She turned upon him like a tigress, striking his great breast with her tiny hands. Tarzan could not understand it." If Tarzan, who was so intimately involved, was baffled, you can imagine my own bewilderment, especially with a donkey engine puffing in my ear. Had the yarn not been so compelling and the chaise longue so comfortable, I would have abandoned both, bearded the Baltimore Chamber of Commerce, and given them my opinion of such a heartless flirt.

171

The Ill-Tempered Clavichord

While one properly expects major characters as vital as Tarzan and Jane to dominate the canvas, it would be grossly unfair to ignore the figures in the background. Professor Archimedes Q. Porter and his secretary carry the burden of the comic relief, and their sidesplitting misadventures evoke chuckles galore. Herewith, for example, is the Professor's tart rejoinder when Philander nervously informs him they are being stalked by a lion: "'Tut, tut, Mr. Philander,' he chided. 'How often must I ask you to seek that absolute concentration of your mental faculties which alone may permit you to bring to bear the highest powers of intellectuality upon the momentous problems which naturally fall to the lot of great minds? And now I find you guilty of a most flagrant breach of courtesy in interrupting my learned discourse to call attention to a mere quadruped of the genus *Felis*. . . . Never, Mr. Philander, never before have I known one of these animals to be permitted to roam at large from its cage. I shall most certainly report this outrageous breach of ethics to the directors of the adjacent zoological garden.'" Can you tie that? The poor boob's so absent-minded he doesn't even realize he's in *Africa*. An equally rich humorous conceit is Esmeralda, the maid, who is constantly "disgranulated" by all the "gorilephants" and "hipponocerouses" about her. I doubt if Amos 'n' Andy at their most inventive have ever surpassed her attempt to soothe Jane at a moment of crisis: "Yas'm, honey, now you-all go right to sleep. Yo' nerves am all on aidge. What wif all dese ripotamuses and man eaten geniuses dat Marse Philander been

172

a-tellin' about—laws, it ain't no wonder we all get nervous prosecution."

Indeed it ain't, and while the subject of nerves is on the tapis, I suspect that at this point in the action Burroughs himself became a trifle discombobulated. With two-thirds of the piece behind him, he still had to unravel Tarzan's complex genealogy, resolve the love story, account for the Professor's treasure (lost and found half a dozen times throughout), and return his puppets intact to everyday life. Accordingly, he introduces a French cruiser to rescue the Baltimoreans and Clayton, and, once they are safely over the horizon, begins untangling the labyrinthine threads that remain. An officer of the vessel, one D'Arnot, has fallen into the clutches of some local cannibals; Tarzan saves the captive and, in return, is taught French, an accomplishment that enables him to translate his father's diary and legally prove himself the real Lord Greystoke. Armed with the proofs, he hurries to America to claim his mate, but Burroughs is just ahead of him, piling up barriers faster than Tarzan can surmount them. Before he can clasp Jane in his arms, he is compelled to rescue her from a Wisconsin forest fire and eliminate her current fiancé, a Scrooge who financed her father's expedition. The minor matter of the treasure is washed up with a check for two hundred and forty-one thousand dollars, which, the ape man fluently explains to Professor Porter, is its market value. And then, as the lovers' last obstacle vanishes, the author, consummate magician that he is, yanks a final bunny from his hat. Jane jilts Tarzan for his cousin,

William Cecil Clayton, and Tarzan, placing her happiness above all, deliberately conceals his true identity. There may be scenes of self-renunciation in Tolstoy that lacerate the heart, but none, I contend, as devastatingly bittersweet as the closing one between the two Greystoke cousins: " 'I say, old man,' cried Clayton. 'I haven't had a chance to thank you for all you've done for us. It seems as though you had your hands full saving our lives in Africa and here. . . . We must get better acquainted. . . . If it's any of my business, how the devil did you ever get into that bally jungle?' 'I was born there,' said Tarzan quietly. 'My mother was an Ape, and of course, she couldn't tell me much about it. I never knew who my father was.' "

ORDINARILY, my fleeting sojourn in such an equatorial mishmash might have had no worse consequences than myopia and a pronounced revulsion from all noble savages thereafter. As luck would have it, though, the Venetian blind above me slipped its moorings as I finished the romance, and, doubtless overstimulated by Tarzan's gymnastics, I climbed up to restore it. Halfway through the process, the cornice gave way and I was left hanging by my fingernails from the picture molding that encircles the room. At this juncture, a certain fourteen-year-old busybody, who has no better means of employing his time than sending postals to shipowners, came snooping into the room. His pitiless gaze travelled slowly from my pendent form to his copy of "Tarzan of the Apes." "Watch out, Buster, you'll strain your milk!" he cautioned. "Better leave that stuff to Weissmuller." Yes, sir, it's pretty disheartening. You lie on your back all day worrying about the junk your children read, you hang from moldings, and that's the thanks you get. It's regusting.

On the Banks of
the Old Hogwash

☞

I CAN'T REMEMBER exactly what my emotions were early last summer when I first grew conscious, in the telepathic way these things happen, that the Chase National Bank was making goo-goo eyes at me. One minute, it was a Hydra-headed, billion-dollar fiscal organization full of impregnable vaults and flinty executives whose basilisk stare probed my wallet and found it picayune; the next, it was twined around me as seductively as a dance-hall hostess in Skid Row, all patchouli, silken ankles, and butterfly kisses, until a red mist swam before me. What made the change of heart so thoroughly inexplicable was the fact that I was just a small, submarginal depositor, and not even a Chase depositor, at that. With the blind, quench-less persistency of a mole, I had hoarded my trifling cache of greenbacks at a branch of the Bobbery & Duplicity Trust Co., drawing out a fiver here, salting a sawbuck there, and never materially bettering my status of finan-cial beachcomber. No scapegrace Australian uncle had ever emerged from Queensland to proclaim me his sole heir, and the one sporting flutter I took on the Irish Hos-pital Sweepstakes netted me a bogus ticket. Yet here was the Chase National, in a couple of exigent newspaper ad-vertisements, tousling my hair and demonstrating its yen for me in the most unbridled fashion. I was flummoxed.

The technique employed to soften me up was based on the principle of contagious enthusiasm; in both cases the advertisements showed photographs of humble Chase de-positors garnished with their ringing testimonials to the bank's liberality and altruism. Under the heading "Young Father Learns Facts," a customer named Kevin Kennedy declared as follows: "When our son arrived, we were kind of stuck for space. So Clara and I decided we had to add on another room, and I went down to the bank for a loan. One thing surprised me quite a bit. All my life I had a notion bankers were kind of close-fisted and cold. Well, I found out that's not true. Fact is, they like to lend money." The interview presumably ended with a giggling, dishev-elled patron being pursued to the sidewalk by a swarm of importunate officials who, amid tearful reproaches, fought to stuff moola into his pockets. Even more fulsome was the testimony of John F. Snodgrass, a Brooklyn architect, whose engaging simper and letter of homage to Chase formed the nub of the second advertisement. "I'm writing this note rather hastily," said Snodgrass, "so forgive all lack of formality, please. I merely want to say thanks for the way you people at Chase Bank have handled my Special Checking Account. I know you don't have to go out of your way to be nice to me, but that courtesy from a 'big fellow' to a 'little fellow'—well, thanks. The way you've treated me has made me very happy, and just in the past week or so, I've told four persons about it. Three were surprised that you bothered about the 'little fellow,' the fourth happened to be an old customer of Chase. He just smiled and said, 'That's how they got that way. They ain't too big to listen or help if and when they can.' I'll drop by one of these days and say thanks." The bank people then took over, and, naturally, they were so happy about Snodgrass's being happy that they blubbered fit to kill. They invited him to come in any old time and help himself to the green stuff lying around the cages, and they implied that if I came in, too, I wouldn't go away empty-handed. At least, that was the way I construed the text, although my glasses were pretty well misted over by then and there may have been some hidden catch to the offer.

AT THE TIME I spotted the foregoing, it occured to me that Chase's competitors would never stand by supinely and let their clientele be shanghaied without a whimper, but I had other fish to fry, and it wasn't until recently that I learned what retaliatory measures had been forced on them. (On Chase's competitors, that is, not on the fish.) The branch of the Bobbery & Duplicity Trust I patronized is situated on lower University Place, under a paper-box factory, and the district, teeming with auction rooms, laundries, invisible-mending shops, and bootblack parlors, can hardly be termed an exotic one. Hence I was altogether unprepared, on arriving at the bank a few mornings ago, for the new, Alhambra-like façade that confronted me. Its cerulean surface was broken by a series of Moorish pillars in low relief, the massive plate-glass windows I remembered had shrunk to two heavily barred grates, and a bull's head spurted water through ceramic nostrils into a wall fountain. Several mischievous beggar boys, straight out of a canvas by Murillo, were gambolling on the pavement and nibbling bunches of grapes.

"Say, *amigos*," I began uncertainly, "didn't there used to be a bank hereabouts?" Their reply was smothered in a burst of Oriental rhythm, and, wheeling toward the entrance, I discovered its source. On a low dais, surrounded by curious passersby, three voluptuous coryphees in the costume of Ouled Naïl dancers were executing a sinuous *danse de ventre* to the strains of "Hindustan," issuing from the brass horn of an old Victor talking machine. A scarlet-faced barker in fancy sleeve garters, whom I distantly recognized as the assistant manager, was exhorting the audience, gesturing toward the interior with his whangee cane.

"Step right up, folks," he invited hoarsely. "Plenty of action going on inside. Need a little transfusion to meet those extra bills? Bailiffs hounding you for back alimony?

179

The Ill-Tempered Clavichord

Pep up your financial glands—we'll put the roses back in that bank account! Hurry, hurry, hurry!"

Hypnotized by his chant, I let myself be drawn inside, where another metamorphosis awaited me. The sprawling maze of partitions that housed the cashiers, tabulating equipment, and fluoroscopes for detecting overdrafts was still intact, but the vestibule had been converted into a torchlit cavern resembling a bodega or an Alice Foote MacDougall restaurant, *circa* 1927. Strings of peppers and onions swung from the ceilings, rustic pottery and gourds decked the walls, and a score of depositors, dotted around hogsheads serving as tables, were drinking sherry and applauding a receiving teller treading a fandango. Suddenly a pair of palms blindfolded me from behind.

"Guess who!" a genial voice boomed in my ear. I turned and beheld Radziwill, the branch manager, his tiny stoat's eyes twinkling. "Well, stranger, it's about time! I thought you'd been run over or switched to Chase or something. Here," he said, masterfully pulling me through a set of bead curtains, "come into the den, where we can talk. How do you like my Turkish corner, eh?"

I gazed around at the welter of Bokhara rugs, taborets, scimitars, and narghiles, and, coughing to clear the incense from my lungs, stammered some inane compliment. Radziwill measured out a thimbleful of arak into a thimble, passed it to me, and ensconced himself on a pouf. "Now, let's have a real heart-to-heart," he coaxed. "Listen, I'm going to lay my cards on the table. Deep down, you've always thought bankers were—well, skinflints, haven't you?"

"Why, of course not," I said loyally. "Look at Haym Salomon, the chap who financed the American Revolution. And Stephen Girard. And Russell Sage."

"Don't try to pull the wool over my eyes," he growled. "You're like all the rest. You think we're ruthless bastards who batten on widows and orphans. Well," he said triumphantly, "this'll show you how wrong you are. How much would it take to make you independent?"

"I've got enough to get by—"

"Huh," he scoffed. "Eating chuck roast instead of porterhouse, wearing rayon underpants instead of silk. You call that living? A man of your stature's entitled to champagne and woodcock, and I intend to see you get it." He fumbled momentarily in his vest and produced two shiny keys.

"Hey, these are real gold!" I exclaimed, testing them with my thumb-nail.

"That's right," he confirmed. "This one fits your new eighteen-room triplex coöperative at Hamster House, Manhattan's most exclusive residential hotel, the deed to which you will find snugly reposing in your safe-deposit box. Its décor is modified Biedermeier, skillfully designed by William Pahlmann to absorb whatever paltry possessions you may wish to remove there. The premises, *ça va sans dire*, are fully staffed, and a world-renowned chef is poised on the ball of his foot ready to tickle your palate with Lucullan viands. To obviate your being plagued by petty distractions, tradespeople will present their account directly to me for settlement."

"Gee whillikers," I murmured, overcome.

"Should you tire of urban pursuits and succumb to the lure of the horizon," continued Radziwill, "the other key may come in handy. It unlocks the ignition of a private twin-diesel yacht, the Wanderola, which is about a block long and lies moored near Sardi's, prepared on your whim to set sail for Samarkand and Ind. She is a veritable floating palace, containing fresh- and salt-water baths, a pianola equipped with ten thousand rolls, and a selection of the latest magazines."

"Radziwill," I said, steadying my voice with an effort, "I'm a plain, homespun sort of cuss, and I want a plain answer. Are you banker or genie?"

"Whatever I am, I'm no skinflint," he replied. "My motto is a square shake for the small depositor. Who knows but tomorrow he may be a real asset to our bank?" I was pocketing the keys with trembling hands when Radziwill, in a movement swift as an adder's, reached over and snatched them from me. "Hold on there, bud," he said incisively. "Don't get any romantic ideas. We're not *giving* you that stuff I mentioned; I was merely dramatizing what our credit facilities could do for you. Now, how small a loan do you need to make your dream come true?"

"Oh," I said. "You mean I'd have to borrow the money from you to pay for it?"

"Sure, if you could cough up the collateral," said Radziwill, his mouth unexpectedly taking on the semblance of a steel trap.

"Maybe I better go home and look over my collateral first," I said uncertainly.

"Do that," he agreed. "And remember, no matter what

headaches you've got, you'll always find a smile awaiting you at B. & D. That's why they call us the Friendlier Bank. *Hasta luego.*" He was escorting me to the curtains when they parted and a pursy gentleman, his mien as imperious as that of the late Collis P. Huntington, strode in. The gleaming silk hat, the checked suit covered with dollar signs, and the unlit Corona between his teeth proclaimed a financial titan not given to brooking interference.

"Confound it, Radziwill," he sputtered. "I've been trying to get you on the wire all morning in regards to that nine-million-dollar loan, as sure as my name is J. Pierpont Midas, but you seem impervious to entreaties. For the last time, will you accept a rate of forty-per-cent interest on said deal?"

"No," said Radziwill boldly, "and for the last time, this exchequer is not tooled up to play lackey to traction magnates, howsoever potent they may be. Get out!"

As THE discomfited plutocrat slunk off promising revenge, the manager dusted his hands. "That's how we treat these *soi-disant* 'big fellows' at B. & D.," he grunted. "It's obscure clucks like you who've nourished our banking system, and if there's any possible way we can repay you—"

"Well, I tell you," I said, opening my billfold. "There might just be. I—I wonder whether you could cash a little check from the gas company. It's a refund for three dollars and ten cents."

"I don't think I understand." A look of almost arctic

hauteur invaded Radziwill's features. "What assurance do we have it's any good, except your word?"

"Their name's lettered on top," I pointed out urgently. "Look, it says 'Consolidated Edison Company—Official Refund Voucher.'"

"Which makes it gilt-edged, of course," Radziwill sneered. "How do I know you didn't run it off at a job printer's? That's a phony if I ever saw one."

"But I've been doing business here fifteen years!" I wailed. "Both my youngsters belong to your Christmas Club. You *must* remember my face!"

"Never saw it before in my life," he said crisply. "Hustle along, now. I've better things to do than quibble with amateur grifters." Ere my mouth had opened to correct his misconception, I was being propelled through an archway into the street. The Ouled Naïls were still doing their grind, but the attention of the crowd wavered automatically as I caromed out and broke my fall on a hydrant. Walking pensively past the houses of Washington Square immortalized by Henry James, I reflected how profoundly banking has altered since his day. Perhaps, I thought, I, too, should adapt to a changing world, and when I got home, I did. I pried out a brick from the fireplace, stowed my anemic savings behind it, and built a pungent blaze out of some institutional ads for a bank. Surprising what fragrance they shed, once you prod them with a match.

A Hepcat
May Look at a King

MICHAEL TODD'S PEEP SHOW, a revue in two acts and
twenty-two scenes, staged and lighted by Hassard Short.
Music and lyrics by Bhumibol (King of Thailand), Prince
Chakraband, Sammy Fain, Herb Magidson, etc., etc.—
From a drama review in the Herald-Tribune.

SCENE: *The Central European branch of Savacool &
Thaumaturge, Ltd., theatrical bookers and artists' repre-
sentatives, in Lausanne, Switzerland. The portion of the
offices observable at rise consists of a somewhat bleak
anteroom furnished with half a dozen spavined chairs and
a spittoon, separated by a low-railed partition from a
switchboard and receptionist's desk. Typing away busily*

185

at the desk is Sibyl Hinshaw, a thin, atrabilious girl on whom years of contact with show folk have acted like an olive press and whose features, together with those of Anna Held and Bernhardt on the walls, have long since become part of the fixtures. The occupants of the ante-room, two in number, offer a marked contrast to its shabby décor. The portly gentleman yawning through a copy of "Variety," who wears a magnificent turban blazing with jewels and a chestful of military orders, bears more than a passing resemblance to the Maharajah of Kapurthala. His companion, more conservatively clad in a frock coat tailored of cloth of gold and trimmed with aigrettes, would not be mistaken east of Suez for anyone but the Nawab of Bhopal. The latter's fingers, incidentally, are so thickly incrusted with emeralds that he is having some difficulty paring his nails. An accordion and a couple of black fibre suitcases, of the sort customarily used by vaudeville performers, lie at their feet.

BHOPAL: Mind you, I won't say this Bhumibol ain't an able administrator, but he don't know a beguine from a cakewalk. The kid is absolutely devoid of rhythm.

KAPURTHALA: He's a Buddhist, that's why. A downbeat don't mean a thing to a Buddhist.

BHOPAL: I'm surprised a showman like Todd would fall for that type air.

KAPURTHALA: Eight to five he's a Buddhist, too. All those guys stick together.

BHOPAL (*carefully lowering his voice*): Well, I heard a story which it may not be gospel but I'll pass it on. You know the skinny monarch who plays the traps at the Café Schlagober? He claims Bhumibol can only write his tunes in the key of C. He's got a little colored fellow in Bangkok that transposes 'em.

KAPURTHALA: Yeah, and I bet he pays him off in fried rice, the chiseller.

BHOPAL: There must be something to it. Why should anybody that their real name is Phumiphon Aduldet suddenly turn around and start calling themselves Bhumibol?

KAPURTHALA: I'll tell you why. So if he gets sued for plagiarism, he's judgment-proof. They're all alike, those kings. The minute they click on Broadway, all they care about is angles.

BHOPAL: I know, but *Bhumibol*—it sounds like a sleeping tablet. If it was Hoagy Bhumibol, or even Blumenthal, you could understand.

KAPURTHALA (*with a shrug*): Go figure out a Siamese. . . . Say, girlie, who do you have to be around here to see Savacool—Genghis Khan? We been waiting an hour.

SIBYL: I've told you already—he's over at the recording studio, cutting a platter.

BHOPAL: Of who?

SIBYL: The Sultan of Morocco, I believe.

BHOPAL: Huh, that groaner! Cliff Edwards in a tarboosh.

KAPURTHALA: Well, there's one thing. Savacool don't have to worry about running out of wax with *that* greaseball around.

BHOPAL: Hey, that's not bad. Maybe we could work it into our routine.

KAPURTHALA: Where we going to play it after we do, at

our boarding house? The bookings Savacool's been getting us, we're lucky to pick up a split week between Antwerp and Kurdistan.

BHOPAL: Look, face facts. The act needs a hypo and there's nothing like dames. Instead of that bit where we jump over our own legs and make with the Indian clubs, I'd like to see some breezy crossfire with a pair of good-looking babes.

KAPURTHALA (*dangerously*): Are you still trying to unload that ten-cent harem of yours?

BHOPAL: Well, after all, they're sitting around the Punjab eating their heads off, and I thought—

KAPURTHALA: Listen, I don't want any of those God-damned gazelle-eyed relatives of yours on my payroll, do you hear me?

BHOPAL: Watch that big mouth, brother. They're *my* concubines, and for two rupees I'd knock those betel-stained teeth right down—

SIBYL: Stop it, both of you! No wonder the managers cancel you left and right! You don't need a hypo; you need a referee.

BHOPAL (*with a growl*): Well, nobody talks to *me* like that. My family descends in an unbroken line—

KAPURTHALA: Descends is right. Sponging as they go.

BHOPAL (*seizing him by the throat*): You'll eat those words, you big pail of lard! (*He releases his grip precipitately as Savacool, a smooth homuncule embodying the less attractive characteristics of Uriah Heep and Simon Legree, enters. He is accompanied by a swarthy young*

188

man with liquid eyes, who is dressed in the resplendent
uniform of a field marshal.*)

SAVACOOL: Here, here, you two, what's cooking?

KAPURTHALA: Nothing—nothing at all. We were just re-
hearsing a new pratfall.

SAVACOOL: Well, throw it away. I got you a real break
at last—the Hedgehog Room of the Piccadilly, in New
York!

BHOPAL: What's that?

SAVACOOL: It's the Wedgwood Room in spades, the place
where all the big-shot producers and movie execs hang
out. They call it the Showcase of Stars. Once they catch
you boys there, you can write your own ticket!

BHOPAL: Does Mike Todd go in there?

SAVACOOL: Go *in* there—he practically sleeps there! I
guarantee you, the minute he sees that mind-reading act
of yours—

KAPURTHALA: But we do a juggling specialty and
nipups.

SAVACOOL: Not any more you don't. From now on,
you're high-class Hindu mystics. You know, reading the
serial number on people's watches, guessing where they
left their umbrella—that is, when you're not waiting on
table, of course.

KAPURTHALA (*picking up his accordion*): Well, you can
suit yourself, Bhopal, but I'll take the Vale of Kashmir.

SAVACOOL (*quickly*): Who runs that?

KAPURTHALA: It's a kind of a Moslem version of Gross-
inger's.

SAVACOOL: Oh, playing cozy, eh? Well, remember this,

bright eyes—whatever it is, I'm entitled to ten-percent commission.

BHOPAL: Good luck. We'll see you in the small-claims court. (*They exit.*)

SAVACOOL (*bitterly*): That's human nature. You run yourself ragged for a couple of hams, and as soon as the wrinkles are out of their cummerbunds, they spit on you. . . . Oh, well. Have a seat, Riza, be with you in a jiffy. Any calls, Sibyl?

SIBYL: Yes. One of the Soong brothers—T.V., I think. He says they're stranded in Liverpool with that plate-balancing act of theirs.

SAVACOOL: I know, I know. And they need money because the Chinaman's holding their laundry.

SIBYL: No, he won't even do it. He doesn't approve of their politics.

SAVACOOL: Well, what am I supposed to do, fly over and wash it for them?

SIBYL: I couldn't tell. The connection was poor and he insisted on talking in the Mandarin dialect.

SAVACOOL: It's pretty fishy. How can T. V. Soong, that he's one of the wealthiest men in the world, be stranded in Liverpool?

SIBYL: You can't fathom those Orientals. They're a race apart. (*Under her breath.*) Who's that over there, a Hapsburg?

SAVACOOL: No, the Shah of Iran. He was laying for me on the sidewalk with a note from Shapiro, Bernstein in New York.

SIBYL: Shall I ask him to leave his ballads and you'll contact him?

SAVACOOL (*magnanimously*): Nah, I'll give him a quick shake. Who knows, maybe the poor *nebich* has something we can peddle. (*Returning to the anteroom.*) O. K., Excellency, you're on the air. Just hum over the lyrics of that novelty you mentioned on the stairs.

SHAH: What do you mean—without a piano or anything?

SAVACOOL: Correct. I'll fill in the sharps and flats in my head.

SHAH: But how can you appreciate all the— well, the tempo and the *lilt* of the song?

SAVACOOL: By instinct, bud—the same way you know if a prime minister is shortchanging you. There's tricks in every trade. Come on, I'll beat time with my foot.

SHAH (*dubiously*): All right, but it's a shame to louse it up. (*He unfurls a roll of music and clears his throat.*)

> 'Way down yonder in Khorramshahr,
> That's where singing and dancing are,
> It's a pleasure to browse there,
> Or so I'm told.
> Persian mamas with shapely gams,
> Lips as sweet as Southern yams—

SIBYL (*breaking in*): Sorry, Mr. Savacool. Leopold of Belgium on the wire.

SAVACOOL: I'll call him back in his dressing room.

SIBYL: He's in some sort of jam; his trunks went astray.

SAVACOOL: Holy cats! (*Jumping up.*) Go on humming, Riza. I'm listening to every word. (*Into phone.*) Yep, speaking. . . . What? . . . You mean with all the trapeze equipment and everything? . . . Oh, *those* trunks. (*With relief.*) What the hell, Leo, you can go on without tights, especially at the matinée. . . . Well, then, borrow a pair of shorts from the stage manager. . . . Positively, by air mail. So long.

SHAH (*continuing undaunted*):

> Take me back to those dreamy glades,
> Let me revel with sloe-eyed maids,
> 'Way down yonder in Khorramshahr.

(*Anxiously.*) How does it strike you, Mr. Savacool?

SAVACOOL: You want my honest reaction, Riza? It's too sophisticated. The average person don't know from the Persian Gulf.

SHAH: Would it be more believable if I made it North Africa? Like:

> 'Way down yonder in Marrakech
> That's the place which it gives me a letch.

SAVACOOL (*concentrating*): No-o-o, I'm groping for some spot—it's on the tip of my tongue. . . . Wait, I got it! What about " 'Way down yonder in New Orleans"?

SHAH: Gee, that'd be sensational!

(*During the foregoing, two individuals swathed in burnooses, but not so heavily as to obscure the fact that they are Ibn-Saud and his son Faisal, have come in. They seat themselves unobtrusively and, realizing they will be forced to wait, draw out a sheep and begin roasting it on a charcoal brazier. Captivated by its delicious odor, Savacool moves toward them like a somnambulist.*)

SAVACOOL: Yes? What can I do for you gents?

IBN-SAUD: Well, it's like this. My boy and I, we've been hashing up a comedy skit. The way we estimate, we have a hundred and fourteen boffs, fifty-six bellies, and twenty-two yocks.

SAVACOOL: Why don't we step into my private office and discuss it over lunch?

FAISAL: We don't want to interrupt you if you're busy.

SAVACOOL (*gaily*): Neighbor, I'm never busy when two guys bust in with a red-hot idea. Here, let me help you carry that stove.

SHAH: Uh—getting back to my lyric, Mr. Savacool, what becomes of the dervish line in the vamp if I make it New Orleans?

SAVACOOL: Yes, yes, work it out along those lines. (*Escorting his new clients off.*) You know, I might just have an opening for two Arab comics in the Hedgehog Room.

SIBYL (*compassionately, as the Shah stands woebegone*): Cheer up, Your Highness. Remember, there's no business like show business.

SHAH: What did you say? Would you mind repeating that? (*She does. An expression of almost insupportable glee invades his face.*) Yowzer! Have I got a terrific theme for a song!

CURTAIN

Hell Hath No Fury...
and Saks No Brake

CB

TELL A WOMAN SHE CAN'T HAVE SOMETHING AND SEE WHAT HAPPENS. . . . Not so long ago we heard about a fine perfume that women are not permitted to buy. Just men. The only way a woman can get the perfume is to be given some. This struck us as being a unique and wonderful idea. So—we looked into Chaqueneau-K . . . smelled it . . . liked it . . . and were convinced you would, too. . . . Thus, we offer Chaqueneau-K to you. For, within an astonishingly short time it has become a sort of legend. Clark Gable buys Chaqueneau-K . . . and Henry Ford II and Angier Biddle Duke and ever so many others whose taste is beyond question . . . to whom gift-giving is an art rather than an obligation. After all, there ought to be something a man can buy for a woman that *she* can't *buy for herself.* Chaqueneau-K will never be sold to a woman.
—*Saks Fifth Avenue brochure.*

194

MRS. HECTOR SEAFORTH PATROON, Park Avenue socialite, prominent Bermuda hostess, and spouse of the chairman of the American Roller Towel Corporation, was in high dudgeon. Stamping her aristocratic foot, shod by Palter DeLiso, she drew her ankle-length Revillon Frères sable coat closer about a statuesque figure sculptured by Lily of France, snapped shut the emerald clasp of her handbag, and glared down majestically at the clerk behind the perfume counter. "Young man," she said with freezing scorn, "do you know, by any remote chance, who you're talking to?"

"Perfectly, Mrs. Patroon," he replied, bowing courteously. "Whether captivating every eye in her ringside box at the Horse Show or brandying persiflage with other celebs at Gotham's gilded '21' Club, the uncrowned queen of the champagne set is class personified, part and parcel of the metropolitan élite. Indeed, 'tis rumored by wiseacres that without her portrait to grace their pages, *Vogue* and *Harper's Bazaar* would long ago be floundering on their derrière."

"Very well, then," retorted the lady, her arctic reserve thawing under his flattery. "Give us a large flacon of Chaqueneau-K and let me have no more ridiculous chin music about you do not cater same to the frail sex."

"I'm sorry, Madam," apologized the clerk. "Those, regrettably, are my orders, that their infraction is punishable by summary dismissal."

"This is the last straw," declared Mrs. Patroon, who was

not accustomed to receiving sauce from myrmidons. "Close my charge accounts as of date, and, I assure you, me and mine will drop dead ere I set another foot in your precious emporium."

As Mrs. Patroon sailed out, head held high, a grizzled old cattleman close by, who had overheard the interchange, chuckled amusedly. "Purty riled, warn't she?" he observed, stroking his tobacco-stained mustache. "Down on the south fork of the Brazos, where I hail from, we know how to curb them fillies." He striped off a picturesque cowboy gauntlet and extended a gnarled finger. "Here, sonny, reckon my missis'd cotton to this—how d'ye call it—Chaknoo?"

"Oh, yes, sir," the clerk said, concealing a smile at the old stager's inept pronunciation. "It's delightfully feminine, a little bit heady—never boring. And she can't buy it for herself, you know—not for a million dollars."

"Pussonally, I'd ruther sniff the ozone a-blowin' through the mesquite than all this fool loco-juice," growled his customer, producing a wad of crumpled bills. "Howsomever, the wimminfolks set rich store by sich fiddledeedee, so I'll be obleeged if ye'll jest draw me off a Mason jar of thet thar shemale nonsense, pardner." The clerk complied with alacrity and, the transaction effected, waved adieu as the patriarch hobbled off on bowed legs. With true Western hospitality, the latter had tendered the salesman his card and a hearty invitation to visit Amarillo. "Maw kin allus bed ye down with the cowpokes, even if'n they don't smell as purty as these dudes," he had cackled, slapping his thigh. The young fellow scanned the card carelessly and was on the verge of pocketing it when a sickening realization smote him. Engraved on it was no homely Lone Star cognomen but the chill legend "The Falcon." A strangled cry burst from his lips. The elusive, mocking creature who had consecrated herself to flouting the pledge that Chaqueneau-K would never be sold to a woman had scored another coup.

"Stop that man—I mean that woman!" the clerk shouted, bounding into the aisle. But it was too late; already the phantom had melted into the crowd, a female David victor once again over the mighty department-store Goliath.

ROBSJOHN CROPSEY, head of the internal-security division of Saks Fifth Avenue, stood at the window of his private sanctum, his lean, saturnine countenance a grim cameo against the twilight. Those who knew him well—and they were few, for the gaunt, loose-jointed Cropsey discouraged intimacy, living only for his work and his daughter Faustine, a graduate student at Columbia U.—might have discerned something almost pantherlike in the man at the moment, the look of a great jungle cat poised to spring. Nor would they have erred; there was a truly feral gleam in his eyes as he wheeled toward the man cringing beside the desk.

"Now, then, Mr. Freytag," he purred. "My dossier reveals that yesterday forenoon you entered our haberdashery and attempted to purchase an Allen Solly cardigan and some Izod hosiery."

"I—I had the money," whimpered Freytag, his face gray with fear.

"That's irrelevant," Cropsey snapped. "You knew these articles were exclusive with Saks, that they were intended for the discriminating few who appreciate the finer things of life." The other nodded miserably. "Other than sheer snobbery, what made you, social cipher and Yahoo that you are, think you had any right to the vestments described?"

Freytag licked his lips. "I wanted to be a big shot," he whined. "I saw Fred Astaire wearing them in a movie, and I figured to be spruce and nobby like him, and—well, I guess I thought I could get away with it." Head in hands, he cowered away from the pitiless gaze and broke into tortured sobs.

"An exterminator," Cropsey lashed him remorselessly. "For this, men herd sheep on the lonely barrens of the Hebrides, women in thatched cottages card and spin their wool, copy writers distill winged words from their hearts' blood—all this so that a vermifuge peddler may pass for Fred Astaire. Well, Freytag, you've gambled and lost. Take him away, boys."

As the luckless wretch was removed by two impersonal operatives in trench coats, condemned to shop at Bamberger's and Loeser's for five long years, Cropsey sank into his chair with a sigh. Always the same, he thought wearily, an unending procession of petty chisellers spawning equally grubby crimes. When would he meet a foeman worthy of his steel? As if in answer to his prayer, Darryl Blauvelt, his second in command and a lad keen as mustard, entered with an aura of suppressed excitement.

"I glean an aura of suppressed excitement, Blauvelt," noted Cropsey, thoughtfully packing shad into his odorous briar. "Out with it, boy." In a few maladroit words, Blauvelt sketched in the salient details of the atrocity at the perfume counter. The scent of burning fish suffused the room as his superior pulled austerely on his pipe. A harsh sound that was less mirth than epiglottal outrage escaped him. "I knew it, by Jove!" he exclaimed triumphantly, squirting a drop of ink into the pipe bowl to extinguish the coals. "Listen—you remember what the clerk told us about Clark Gable, Henry Ford II, and Angier Biddle Duke?"

"Why, yes," said Blauvelt, racking his memory. "He noticed that Gable wore a domino mask and Inverness cape when he came in, that Mr. Ford had a billycock hat and muttonchop whiskers, and that Duke was sporting burnt-cork makeup and a rhinestone vest. We thought it was odd at the time—"

"Odd!" exploded Cropsey. "Great Scott, man, don't you see? Impostors all! It was the Falcon, now revealed to be a past-mistress of disguise, who fobbed off her bogus charge plates! Do we have snaps of the trio to check my conjecture?"

"We do, sir," confirmed the other, extracting them instanter from a drawer cunningly concealed in the wall. "The average public would be floored to learn that our files are as comprehensive as Scotland Yard's." A single glance corroborated the chief's deduction; except for the hirsute appendage edging the film star's lip, the three were clean-cut men of distinction, devoid of ostentatious garb.

A muscle twitched in Cropsey's cheek and a dangerous yellow light shone in his gritted teeth. "A crafty adversary, this, Blauvelt," he rapped out. "Somewhere in that vast beehive of humanity, the Falcon has gone to earth, storing up venom for another pounce. We've got to match her woman's guile with the very snare she used on us. Attend me carefully. . . ."

FAUSTINE CROPSEY stirred her tea dreamily and, lowering the newspaper that shielded her piquant face, cast a wary glance around the restaurant. Save for two or three matrons hissing confidences over their jelly rolls, and the waitress yawning nearby, the Forty-sixth Street Schrafft's was deserted. She nervously consulted her watch, wondering what mischance could have delayed her contact. Through office and factory, library and rehearsal hall, word had sped from one woman to another in the network of the L.C.M.S.—the League to Combat Male Supremacy —that the Falcon was in peril and was to receive briefing at the third table along the north wall of the tearoom at five-fifteen that afternoon. Considering their devious routing, the tidings had travelled with amazing speed. They could have been telephoned to her just as easily, but then, reflected Faustine, the machinery of conspiracy always functions ponderously. She had cause to know. It had been whilst penning her thesis on the machinery of conspiracy at Columbia that Chaqueneau-K had hurled its defi at her sex. The insolent mandate proscribing the scent had lashed Faustine to fury; in a flash of resentment, the idea of the avenging sisterhood was born. Fanned by general indignation, it had grown overnight into a widespread cabal that enabled its leader, under the *nom de guerre* of the Falcon, to execute her intrepid forays. All Manhattan was agiggle at the sham Texan who had circumvented the edict, yet some vague premonition, a fear that she had over-reached herself, was chewing at Faustine.

"Chicken giblets with orange snow, and a small pandowdy." The words, uttered in a swift undertone, cut sharply into her reverie. It was the password; unperceived by Faustine, her contact had slipped into the chair behind. As the waitress scribbled the order and moved off, Faustine, lips barely moving, whispered the countersign: "Pandowdy, Roger, and over."

"You are the Falcon?"

"I am known by that name. I have others."

"I caught a glimpse of your profile when I sat down. Your hair's terribly unattractive."

"You're no bargain yourself. What message do you bring?"

"I speak through a doily. Pay close heed. A perfume exists at the vigil counter."

"Is the message in code?" asked Faustine. "I don't follow. Repeat, please."

"Sorry. A vigil exists at the perfume counter. Tread

softly; gins and pitfalls are being prepared. Swoop with care, Falcon. More I may not say."

"Why not?"

"My mouth is full of corn bread. Wait till I swallow."

The organization was becoming unwieldy, Faustine decided. Instructions would have to be issued to contacts to do their eating off duty. Aloud, she said, "Anything else?"

"Yes." Desperate urgency underlined the other's voice. "It is like thrusting your head into the lion's maw to venture into that store, even to one of your cool bravado who her aplomb might well be ruffled by scores of dicks subjecting you to their pitiless scrutiny."

"Hmm." Faustine's mouth tightened. "You are certain nobody followed you here?"

"They may have. Some fresh egg in the subway kept pinching me, but he got off at Columbus Circle."

"That's all." Her chieftain withdrew into her paper. "You can go now."

"What about my giblets?"

"They seem normal," said the Falcon cryptically, "but if I were you, I'd consult a physician about my adenoids."

"CAN YOU DIRECT ME to the perfume counter, please?" The speaker, a swarthy, autocratic individual in flowing burnoose, whose curled black beard, snowy turban, and bejewelled yataghan bespoke the baking deserts of Trans-

Jordan, stood irresolute in the turmoil of the brassière section. The salesgirl at his elbow, though inured to the grotesque by her environment, blinked in momentary surprise.

"Oh, yes, sir. Two aisles over and left," she said, and smiled coquettishly. "You speak surprisingly good English for a lint-head."

"Thanks," the man acknowledged with Old World gallantry. "On account of my governor was well off, I was senior wrangler at Brasenose. *Salaam aleikum.*" He strode off, spurs jangling, amid a battery of languishing glances. As he gained his objective, several workmen who had been deployed about polishing showcases and spearing excelsior abandoned their labors and drifted nearer.

"A dozen bottles of Chaqueneau-K, my good woman," the Arab said to the angular spinster in black behind the counter, "and do not spare full measure, lest the gazelles in my harem accuse me of favoritism."

The saleswoman surveyed him coolly out of a lean, saturnine countenance, removed the briar from between her teeth, and signalled the workmen to hold themselves at the ready. "Well, Falcon, we meet at last," she said, in the rasping Cropsey nasal that had spelt curtains to many a trickster's career. "Nab her, men!" In a trice, Cropsey's aides had closed in, pinioned their prize, and borne the captive, kicking and struggling, into the freight elevator. So deftly was the incident staged that not a head turned to remark it, most of the shoppers dismissing it merely as a strenuous preparation for the midseason white sales.

The Ill-Tempered Clavichord

HALF AN HOUR LATER, Cropsey, feet on desk and shad in pipe, reviewed the affair for his admiring subordinate in half a dozen broad strokes. "The Falcon, emboldened by success, was cock-a-hoop," he explained negligently. "Hence, foolhardiness and concomitant disaster. It was child's play."

"I know, sir," cut in Blauvelt, "but the thing is, I'm afraid we pinched the wrong—"

"Don't interrupt," reproved Cropsey. "I was observing that my modest knowledge of criminal psychology—"

"Please, sir," the younger man persisted. "I feel I've got to tell you. That sheik was legit. We tried to rip his beard off, but all we have is a lawsuit." As his dumbstruck senior goggled at him, there was an insistent knocking on the door. Blauvelt peered out and engaged in a low-pitched colloquy. "No, no, he's tied up," he said with finality. "You what? . . . From where? . . . Well, I'll see." He looked uncertainly over his shoulder at Cropsey, sunk in a blue funk. "There's a—a Mennonite gentleman here, from Lancaster County, sir. He says it's something urgent —about Chaqueneau-K."

Cropsey beckoned abstractedly. A small, plump figure clad in the sober raiment of the Pennsylvania sect, his beaver hat shading a visage set off by a luxuriant chin whisker, insinuated himself into the room. Rubicund cheeks glowing like Winesaps with embarrassment, he laid a gift-wrapped bottle on the blotter.

"You take back from me this perfume, not?" he implored. "I will be so grateful. My wife will bake for you a shoo-fly pie—"

"Blauvelt! Who is this man?" Cropsey half rose. "We don't make refunds here!"

"*Nein, nein,* you shall have it as a present," the visitor said doggedly. "Keep it for a souvenir. Give it to your daughter."

"Souvenir?" Cropsey grated. "Daughter? What do you know of my daughter?"

"Ha-ha!" his vis-à-vis rejoined, with a sly grin. "I know one thing, old smearcase. She has a *Dummkopf* for a father."

"Damn your impudence, sir!" Cropsey went white with passion and snatched a penang-lawyer from the wall. "I'll teach hayseeds to come in here and insult me!" His hand recoiled from the intruder's collar as a mocking feminine voice rang out from beneath the beaver hat.

"Not so fast, Daddy," it warned. "Two can play at that game!" With a dexterous movement, the Mennonite swept off hat and beard, shook out a mop of honey-colored hair, and disclosed to the electrified sleuth his treasured off-spring.

"Faustine!" choked her sire. "You—the Falcon?"

"The same," returned the girl, violet orbs flashing defiance. "Just a normal, spunky miss pitting her wiles against consuming odds to deflate the bumptious masculine ego."

"Well, I'll be—jiggered!" gasped Darryl, thoroughly flabbergasted. "She certainly took me in."

"And me, too," concurred Cropsey, his sportsman's code

bowing to the inevitable. "This has been a good lesson to all concerned that male chauvinism is un-American to the core. From here in, Blauvelt," he announced inflexibly, "this store will stand as a bastion against sexual niggling, freely retailing Chaqueneau-K to every gender."

"Dear old Dad!" approved Faustine, enveloping him in a bear hug. "I really believe you knew the Falcon's identity from the start, you old fox."

"Well, best leave sleeping dogs lie," Cropsey twinkled. "As for you two young scalawags, do not imagine I have been blind to the sheep's eyes exchanged behind my back, and the furtive smooching. She's yours, my boy," he told Blauvelt as the blushing pair sought each other's arms. "And now, if you will excuse me, I will buzz on down to the Gamecock and buy a glass of oblivion for a suspicious frog in my throat." The lovers stood clasped in the gloaming and watched him go. He turned with a whimsical smile on the threshold. "After all," he said, and for an instant elf overrode detective, "there ought to be something a man can buy for a frog that a frog can't buy for itself." And he shut the door very carefully.

Our Vines Have Shrewder Grapes

I DON'T SUPPOSE THAT, sibling for brainpan, there was a single layman in the whole borough of Manhattan the other night whose thoughts were further from anthropology than mine. Outside of spearing an olive in a Martini, shrinking my head slightly in the ambient fluid, and drumming on the radiator to exorcise the television in the apartment below, I was as remote from primitive cultural patterns and unaware of the science that concerns itself with them as one could possibly be. In other words, I was living in a first-class fool's paradise equipped with *chauffage central* and *confort moderne*, and anybody with the merest knowledge of anthropological sporting odds could have predicted that sooner or later I was a cinch to be evicted. It took an unconventional bailiff to oust me—a lady ethnologist in an amusement weekly, of all things—but when I had finished dusting myself off, I was tuned in to a scientific wave length I'd never really heard before.

The lady responsible was Dr. Margaret Mead, associate curator of ethnology at the Museum of Natural History, and the journal in which her provocative statement appeared was *Cue*, whose theatre calendar I was consulting at the time. I had heard repeated hosannas for a play called "Copts and Jobbers," which dealt with the wholesaling of scarabs by an early Egyptian sect and which held forth the promise of a stirring evening's entertainment. Unfortunately, it must have flopped out of town at Khartoum, or perhaps King Farouk had earmarked its ingénue for palace use; at any rate, my quest ultimately fetched me up against an article on Dr. Mead by Ruth Hawthorne Fay, one of a series about women who have made important contributions to New York life. The major part of it was given over to Dr. Mead's public career, her field trips to faraway places, her working habits, and her essential femininity, none of it calculated to set one plunging in his stall, but the last paragraph lassoed my wandering attention. "She is married to Gregory Bateson, an Englishman and a distinguished anthropologist," the text disclosed. "The Batesons have a ten-year-old daughter, Catherine, who so far has shown no particular leanings toward anthropology. 'She may, though,' her mother remarks. 'She has an observing eye. I've a dress that's faintly Renoir in design. When I put it on the other morning, she said, "Mother, you need a little parasol to go with it." So far as I know, she's never seen a parasol, unless it's in a picture at school. But that's how we anthropologists learn to look at life. It's a combination of the scientific method and disciplined intuition—fitting bits and pieces together until a pattern of the whole emerges.' "

If Franz Boas, Malinowski, and the eminent curator herself had leaped into the room clad in black leotards and formed a living pyramid, I could not have been more electrified, for that paragraph brought into sudden focus a number of events in my own family that had been puzzling me over the past winter. Neither of my children, despite their exposure last spring to two of Dr. Mead's favorite seedbeds, New Guinea and Bali, has shown any greater penchant for anthropology than Catherine. They tend, in fact, to treat their sojourn in Indonesia as if it had been an attack of herpes zoster, a vaguely shameful episode that alienated them from society and is best excused by pretending abysmal ignorance. When questioned about such everyday places as Celebes and the Moluccas, for instance, they invariably dummy up, or, if pressed, locate them between Denver and Salt Lake. Ask them to describe the simplest Balinese ceremony, like the daily ritual of spitting on Dutch hotel-keepers, and the cat's got their tongue.

Consequently, I was caught off balance somewhat a couple of months ago when my son, who I thought was quietly freezing his marrow with a comic published by Charnel House, edged into the living room and began with cold objectivity to analyze a party we had given the night before. There had been nothing exceptional about it; two playwrights had accused each other of plagiarism and been quelled without loss of hemoglobin to either, and one of the older business girls had broken the dumb-waiter cord in an attempt to duplicate Lillian Leitzel's gymnastics. But no greenstick fracture, stabbing, or domestic showdown had marred the evening, and everyone, even the fair acrobat, had cleared in no apparent need of a jury rig. The boy felt, nonetheless, that the soirée had fallen short in some indefinable respect. He groped to put it into words that kept eluding him.

"The shrimp? The cypress shavings flavored with curry?" I prompted. "I can't think what else it could have been except the liquor."

"That's it, that's it!" he said eagerly. "The people were drinking the punch with their hands—like this." He cupped his palms and scooped them up toward his face, graphically illustrating how the liquid had dribbled down over the guests' corsages and shirt fronts. "I don't know—it didn't seem right to me."

"But that's the only way you can get it out of the bowl," I explained patiently. "Don't you see, there's a gap between the surface of the hooch, so to speak, and the mouth—"

"Couldn't you use a beaker or an Erlenmeyer flask or something?" he suggested. "Some kind of a little vessel to decant the punch from the bowl?"

"By George, I never thought of that before," I murmured thoughtfully. "A regular cup for the purpose, eh?" I was on the verge of interrogating the lad to ascertain whether he had seen anything of the sort in his school-books, but, remembering that he never opened them, I forbore. To be candid, I was just a shade jealous of the ease with which he had evolved a concept that had baffled older heads for years. For a fleeting moment, I had the uncomfortable suspicion that I was nourishing a viper in my bosom. Had I sniffed the air keenly, though, I would have detected the unmistakable whiff of ether that meant I had been present at the birth of an anthropologist.

ABOUT A WEEK LATER, as I was passing the local florist shop, Batrachian, the proprietor, bade me a civil good evening and said he hoped the rubber plant was proving satisfactory. Presuming that he had slipped a cog, since I had noticed no such ornament around the house, I assured him it was flourishing and went my way. The significance of his words came home to me at dinner. In the midst of the usual peevish threnody that accompanied the meal, I overheard my daughter snivelling. Her brother had promised to contribute equally to the cost of a rubber plant but had welshed.

"You mean you actually *bought* a rubber plant?" I exclaimed, my voice soaring into the alto register. "For Christmas' sake, what would possess any rat—"

"Please, can't we bring down the pitch a trifle?" implored my wife. "The maid can drop the roast by herself without an offstage cue."

"Any rational person to want a rubber plant?" I de-

manded, unheeding. "Next thing you know, we'll have a
dado, a mission table with a calfskin on it, and a pianola.
Whose idea was it?"

"The children's," she said. "They haven't told me why,
but if they're willing to spend their allowance on it, there
must be a reason."

The logic of this assumption seemed assailable, and I
proceeded to assail it, without, however, deriving a clue
to the purpose of the plant. That remained an enigma for
almost a month, during which time I discovered that it
was the hub of all kinds of mysterious activity. Diagonal
slits were cut in the bark and a bucket suspended below
them, sinister gurgling and boiling sounds issued through
my son's locked door, and the premises unaccountably
took on the hot, steamy languor of a Malayan plantation.
One bitter January morning, while girding myself to face
the snow and slush in the streets, I noticed the children
eying me expectantly.

"Why don't you put something on your feet to keep
them dry?" asked my daughter, as casually as Cameo
Kirby proposing a round of stud to a wealthy cattle drover.

"Like what?" I returned. "As far as I know, there's no
method of protecting the extremities in the manner you
indicate. Unhappily, luckless mankind appears destined
to fall victim to coryza, rhinitis, and a host of respiratory
ills from the vicissitudes of these northerly climes, not
only shortening tempers but robbing business of untold
manpower hours."

"Well, these may provide a partial solution," she said
diffidently, producing from behind her back a pair of

crude homemade galoshes, or arctics. I could hardly credit my ears when I learned they had been fashioned entirely by hand; even the clasps, paltry and imperfect as they were, had been snipped out of tin cans and laboriously riveted to the canvas uppers, the whole being stained with lampblack to simulate an old-fashioned rubber boot. That juvenile fingers could fabricate so complex a piece of footgear was in itself astounding, but what really moved me was the children's utter modesty about their achievement. They had never seen an overshoe in Bali or New Guinea, certainly; I now realize they had merely applied the disciplined, intuitive approach characteristic of the budding anthropologist and *reasoned* it into existence. Yet they claimed no special genius or inspiration, nor, indeed, were they piqued that I never wore their handiwork, preferring to keep it in our curio cabinet alongside the Papuan pressure cooker I picked up on Thursday Island.

THIRTEEN YEARS of fatherhood should have warned me that once the trial balloon succeeded, another ascension was inevitable. It was the sight of the fat-tailed sheep in the foyer, I guess, that convinced me we had ceased being a family and had become a cottage industry. Having established, by a few adroit and seemingly offhand questions, that the animal really belonged to us and had not strayed in from a neighbor's apartment, I deliberately ignored its presence and waited for events to take their natural course.

As the days drew on, the youngsters were swept up in a cycle of handicraft as colorful as a Scottish crofter's. With the aid of a borrowed collie, the sheep was rounded up and sheared, the wool combed and carded, and a rough hand loom improvised—the collie, of course, contributing invaluable advice at every stage of the process. Ofttimes of an evening, lounging by the radio, my wife and I could hear our daughter tonelessly humming Thomas Hood's "The Song of the Shirt" to herself as she sat cross-legged on her bed and patiently plied her needle; the boy, bent over his miniature lathe, was absorbed in polishing some type of rude bone objects that looked like buttons.

"You know," remarked my wife at length with a frown, "I have a hunch those two are up to something in there— fabric-wise, I mean. Remember your old tuxedo pants I threatened to discard not long ago?"

"The ones that were dimly Degas in feeling?"

"Yes." She nodded. "Well, just as I was discarding them, the kids stopped me and said that what you needed was a little tartan dinner jacket like the Duke of Windsor wears to go with them." She held up her Tom Collins and regarded it speculatively against the light, watching the shimmering interplay of ice and fruit. "I wonder if—"

"Don't be an ass," I said. "Why, they've never even seen the Duke of Windsor. You're always reading between the limes." It was an unfortunate taunt domestic-wise, for, woman-wise, her instinct proved superior to mine man-wise.

Forty-eight hours afterward, I found awaiting me among my birthday presents an authentic tartan dinner coat, cut and sewn with an artistry not commonly seen this side of Savile Row—or the other, for that matter. Though the children accepted my encomiums with pardonable pride, they made it clear that the entire garment, from design to execution, had originated in their own resourceful imaginations. "We just felt Windsor would wear a thing like that, so why not a perfect prince like Daddy?" they argued. "Hence, we started in from scratch with the sheep and explored every avenue until we got what we wanted."

WELL, Dr. Mead, there it is—a chain of circumstances that may strike the secular mind as unusual, but if any doubting Thomas can come up with a better explanation to fit the facts than yours, I'm ready to listen to it. I can always be reached care of the Mangrove Trading Corp., Ternate, North Moluccas, Indonesia, when I'm out of New York, and, judging from the way things have been breaking recently at the flat, I expect to be out of New York a good deal. Happy curating, and before I forget, one further question: How old does an anthropologist have to be to get his working papers?

Swing Out,
Sweet Opiate

☞

MUSIC with anesthesia has been installed in the University of Chicago clinics to help alleviate tension of patients undergoing surgery. Used with spinal, local, or regional anesthesia, the music is piped to the operating rooms from a central recorder room where three duo-channel magnetic tape recorders of classical, semiclassical, and popular music play continuously for four hours. The patient and the anesthesiologist, who proctors the program, hear the music through lightweight, stethoscope-type earphones.

Music for surgery is not a new idea. Surgeons have reported in medical literature on the success of the use of phonograph and radio in operating rooms.

—*Science Magazine.*

SCENE: *An operating room in an up-to-date metropolitan hospital. In contrast to the marmoreal décor of the aver-*

age surgery, this is a warm, inviting chamber, designed to soothe patient and technician alike—blush-pink walls, wheat-colored instrument closets, and an autoclave of intense Veronese green. The windows facing the exterior and the corridors embody the newest wrinkle in optical research; instead of the occupants enjoying full vision without being seen, as heretofore, they cannot look out and are exposed to any busybody who cares to rubber in at them. At rise, Miss Kipness, a nurse, and Prather, an anesthesiologist, both wearing earphones, are absorbed in routine tasks. Miss Kipness, laboriously turning a blacksmith's grindstone, is whetting a tray of scalpels while Prather kneels before a tank of nitrous oxide, mending a stubborn leak with court plaster. The tank, like those displayed in movie shorts in which chimpanzees enact human roles, bears the legend "Laughing Gas" in white block letters. Apparently the gas defies Prather's efforts to confine it, for he utters an exclamation of annoyance, strips off the adhesive, and seals the leak with a wad of gum.

PRATHER (*dusting his knees*): There, that'll hold till after lunch. I'll bring back my jackknife and whittle a plug.

MISS KIPNESS: You could use this lancet, for all the good it'll ever be now. I wish Dr. Ribblesdale wouldn't beat time on the patients when he works.

PRATHER: Well, between you and me, Kipness, he operates in the wrong tempo. You can't do a decent tonsillectomy to a boogie-woogie. A strangulated hernia, yes, but

217

for nose and throat you want strings—something with schmaltz.

MISS KIPNESS: I know. That's where Malahide Purdy was a genius. Did you ever work with him?

PRATHER: German Deaconess Hospital in Chicago, wasn't he?

MISS KIPNESS: Yes. He always used to take his cue from the music. Like if he was doing a mastoid to a Sousa march and the rhythm changed to a samba, he'd switch to another part of the patient just like *that*.

PRATHER: The same with Gouverneur Foltis. I'll never forget one time, up at the Mayo, when he was trepanning a senator and the Goodman sextet was playing "After You've Gone"—

MISS KIPNESS (*shushing him*): Oh-oh, listen to this riff of Tommy Dorsey's. It's angelic. Joe Bushkin at piano and Cozy Cole on the traps.

PRATHER: Mmm, not bad. That might blend very nicely with cyclopropane the next time we have to do a nerve block.

MISS KIPNESS: Have you ever thought of using barbital and a banjo version of "Turkey in the Straw" together? Somebody like Mike Pingitore or Eddie Peabody.

PRATHER: Well, when it comes to hypnotic percussion, you can't top Gene Krupa and five cc.s of Majondie solution (*Reminiscently*) Remember Gene in the old Madhattan Room of the Pennsylvania—"Diga-Diga-Doo" and "Bambalina"? He used to mesmerize the joint with some phrase he kept mumbling over and over under his breath.

MISS KIPNESS (*nodding*): "Ham and eggs and *some* pork

chops." I still don't understand how he kept his mind on two things at once. He'd have made a wonderful surgeon. (*A white-jacketed orderly enters, pushing a carriage on which a man named Veblen is recumbent. The patient's color is good and his breathing untroubled, but his eyeballs show a tendency to roll in his head, possibly because of his unfamiliar surroundings.*)

ORDERLY: *Emergency*—Dr. Imbrie phoned in to admit him. He'll be along any minute.

MISS KIPNESS: Where's his chart?

ORDERLY: It blew down the elevator shaft on my way up here. The engineer's in there trying to find it, but it may take a while.

MISS KIPNESS: Ah, skip it. We don't really need it. It's only so the resident can show off when he makes his rounds. (*Orderly exits; she turns to Veblen.*) Now lie back like a good boy and don't peer at all those fiendish instruments. What's wrong, touch of coronary or something?

VEBLEN (*muffled*): Uh-uh. I—I swallowed a foreign body.

MISS KIPNESS: What, a fishbone? (*Veblen shakes his head.*) Your dental plate? . . . Speak up, man, we're not mind readers.

VEBLEN: A golf ball. I swallowed a golf ball by accident.

PRATHER (*sotto voce*): Psychosomatic. Probably gulped down some indigestible, rubbery food in a hurry and dreamed up the ball as a convenient scapegoat.

VEBLEN: I tell you I *did*—I feel it resting on me like a stone! You wait till Dr. Imbrie brings the X-ray. You'll see.

MISS KIPNESS (*indulgently*): You're quite sure you didn't

have a hot pastrami sandwich with cream soda? Think back.

VEBLEN: Well, not with cream soda. Celery tonic.

PRATHER: There, what'd I tell you?

VEBLEN: But that was over two weeks ago. The business with the diabolo set was just last night.

PRATHER: The diabolo set? (*Delicately*) I think we'd better find his chart, Kipness. I have an idea this feather merchant belongs in some other wing.

VEBLEN (*desperately*): I can prove it by my family— they all saw it! I was cleaning out my golf bag, and the kids found the diabolo in the hall closet. While I was demonstrating how to balance it on the string, I put this Kro-flite ball I was holding in my mouth for a second—

MISS KIPNESS (*placating him*): Of course. It happens all the time. Now relax, think about your bills or the war.

VEBLEN (*not to be diverted*): If I had a little round object, I'd show you. What's that in your pocket? (*Miss Kipness produces a ping-pong ball from her apron, which, by a slight dramatic coincidence, she has picked up in the nurses' recreation room. She and Prather exchange skeptical smiles as Veblen places it between his lips and pantomimes the mishap.*)

PRATHER: O.K., O.K. We'll take your word for it. (*Suddenly Veblen gasps and the ball disappears. An electric pause. Prather thoughtfully scratches his nose.*) Well, at least we've got something to go on now.

VEBLEN: I—I'm all congested . . . some water . . .

MISS KIPNESS (*clapping her earphones to his head*):

Here, breathe in slowly and listen to the music. That better?

VEBLEN (*struggling*): I don't want Muggsy Spanier. I want Dr. Imbrie. (*His appeal bears fruit; the door opens and the physician, face scarlet and hair dishevelled, hastens in.*)

IMBRIE: Sorry, folks—picked up a nail on the way over and had to change the flat myself. Ah, there you are, Veblen. All cozy? We'll have you skipping rope before you can say Jack Suffocation.

VEBLEN: Gee, Doc, I'm in awful shape. You'll never guess what happened.

IMBRIE (*gaily adjusting earphones*): Don't tell me you went and swallowed another ball.

VEBLEN: That's right—a ping-pong ball. Ask these people if I didn't.

IMBRIE (*owlishly*): You mean you swallowed it since you came in here? . . . Well, now, that's a serious charge and we'll have to check into it. How about it, Prather?

PRATHER (*with a wink*): Well, sir, Mr. Veblen's a bit upset, naturally—

IMBRIE: And I don't blame him. I tell you, when I saw his X-ray this morning, I said to myself, "Bye-bye, Veblen, old boy!" (*Veblen's fingers dance uncontrollably.*) Where *is* that X-ray, by the way?

MISS KIPNESS: Didn't you bring it with you?

IMBRIE: Damn and blast, I must have left it on the curb. I used it to keep the jack from slipping. Oh, well, no matter. We'll drop a bronchoscope into him and snake out that ball as easy as shooting fish in a barrel.

MISS KIPNESS: We don't have our 'scope handy, Doctor. The interior decorator's replating it to harmonize with the fixtures.

IMBRIE: Botheration, this must be my unlucky day. Well, I'll just have to rig up a wire loop, something like a little quahog rake. (*He sets to work.*) Nurse, sponge off the patient's forehead, he seems to be dehydrating.

PRATHER: Too bad you're not ready to roll, sir. Knockout arrangement of "Ol' Man River" on here by André Kostelanetz.

IMBRIE: I don't like a ballad for this particular technique. A good, lively jump tune expands the pharynx beautifully.

VEBLEN (*apprehensively*): Look, Doc, aren't—aren't you going to scrub up, the way they usually do?

IMBRIE: You've been seeing too many medical movies, Veblen. What's the trouble, got a germ phobia? All set. Pinpoint the area with a flashlight.

MISS KIPNESS: The battery's dead in mine, Doctor. Do you mind if I hold up a match instead?

IMBRIE: No, but careful you don't scorch his nose. Stand by with the procaine, Prather. "Twelfth Street Rag"—perfect. When I count three, pick it up on the downbeat— (*He breaks off, listens intently.*) What happened?

PRATHER (*blanching*): The music's conked out.

MISS KIPNESS: It can't—not at a time like this!

IMBRIE: Steady, don't lose your heads. (*The public-address system crackles.*) Here comes a bulletin.

VOICE: Attention, all operative units. A small electric filament, which it is inextricably yoked up with the central amplifier, is on the fritz. We urgeon the surgeons—correction, please—doctors, do not proctor until further notice. Scalpels down. That is all.

IMBRIE (*hotly*): Human lives in the balance and they expect me to quit, do they? I'll show 'em! Many's the time my granddad operated on a kitchen table by lamplight, with only chloroform and an old harmonium at his elbow.

PRATHER: We're in there with you, chief! What do we do?

IMBRIE (*rolling up his sleeves*): Boil some water, and lots of it!

MISS KIPNESS: But we've oodles of hot water, more than we need.

IMBRIE: Hmm, that's right. Let me think. Have you a comb? (*She plucks one from her hair.*) Good. Stretch a piece of Kleenex across it and start singing. I don't care what, just belt it out. Ready, Prather?

PRATHER: Say when, sir.

IMBRIE: One, two, three! (*As Miss Kipness strikes up "Basin Street Blues" and the trio converges on Veblen, atavism rears its fortuitous head. He squirms off the table like an eel, bounds out the door like a cheetah, and heads for a conjur man.*)

CURTAIN

Four-and-Twenty Blackjacks

⊂⊅

THE MINUTES of the Oxford Union for 1920—a copy of which is, of course, readily available at everyone's elbow —reveal that during its entire winter session that world-famed discussion group and conventicle of pundits was sunk in a mood of almost suicidal despair. The honourable members, thitherto scornful of American eloquence, had become so alarmed at the rhetoric stemming from the Classical High School Debating Society in Providence, Rhode Island, that they were seriously considering mass hara-kiri. "What is the sense of we tongue-tied slobs beating our gums," lamented one Balliol man, summing up the universal sentiment, "when these brilliant Yank speechifiers in faraway New England, every man jack of them a Cicero or Demosthenes, has made a chump out of us oratory-wise?" His defeatism was well grounded; week after week, in a series of dazzling intramural debates, the Rhode Island striplings were exhibiting a fluency rivalling that of Edmund Burke and the elder Pitt on such varied topics as "Resolved: That the Philippines Be Given Their Independence," "Resolved: That the End Justifies the Means," and "Resolved: That the Pen Is Mightier Than the Sword." It was a great natural phenomenon, as inexplicable as parthenogenesis or the strapless bra, and I still feel cocky that I should have presided over it as chairman of the society—well, chairman pro tem, which is almost the same thing. The descendants of Roger Williams don't go in for lousy little distinctions.

The club met every Wednesday afternoon in a classroom that generations of adolescent males had endowed with the reek of a pony stable. It shied a·few erasers about to insure a proper concentration of chalk dust in the lungs, and then, as an apéritif to the polemics, listened to an original paper read by one of the membership. Most of these treatises were on fairly cosmic themes; I myself contributed a philippic entitled "Science vs. Religion," an indigestible hash of Robert Ingersoll and Haldeman-Julius, in which I excoriated the Vatican and charged it, under pain of my displeasure, to mend its ways before our next meeting. Occasionally, somebody would alter the pattern and deliver an essay in lighter vein, on, say, "The Witchery of Jack Frost" or "Squeteague Fishing."

Though parliamentary procedure was mother's milk to

me, and it was self-evident that I was marked out for political leadership, an altogether fortuitous circumstance scotched my career. One afternoon, while refereeing a tedious forensic battle on the single tax, I somehow lost the thread and became absorbed in a book about a gentleman cracksman called "The Adventures of Jimmie Dale," by Frank L. Packard. To this day, I cannot account for my psychological brownout; I assume it sprang from the heavy burden of administrative anxieties I was carrying. At any rate, enthralled with the melodrama, I did not discover that the meeting had adjourned until I found Mr. Bludyer, the principal, shaking me violently. He told me that various restoratives, among them my own gavel, had been tried on me without effect and that finally I had been cashiered. "I'd take up some pastime that doesn't tax the intellect, like volleyball," he suggested pointedly. That I went on to score notable gridiron successes and overnight become the idol of the school is unimportant. It was only when the B. M. C. Durfee High School, of Fall River, kayoed us on the issue "Resolved: That Cigarette Smoking Is Injurious to Our Youth" that my rueful colleagues realized the price they had paid for their inconstancy.

QUITE RECENTLY, at Kaliski & Gabay's auction parlors, I was whipsawed into buying Packard's fable as part of a job lot of second-hand books, and, faced with the dilemma of rereading it or being certified as a spendthrift incapable of handling his own funds, I chose the coward's way. Before I could get into the story, though, I was sidetracked by the publisher's advertisement in the flyleaves, a sample of the quaint propaganda used in 1917 to popularize the habit of reading. There was nothing like reading, affirmed the A. L. Burt Company, "for a hardworking man, after his daily toil, or in its intervals. It calls for no bodily exertion." The statement may have been true of the four hundred titles that followed, but not of "The Adventures of Jimmie Dale." Its previous owner had apparently read it while sipping mucilage, for whole episodes were gummed together in the most repulsive fashion. Between prying them apart with a fruit knife, geeing up the fragments, and retrieving the book from the wastebasket, into which it unaccountably kept sliding like a greased pig, I was almost as pooped as the time I whitewashed a three-room henhouse singlehanded.

To anyone who has ever worked his way out of a boxwood maze, the plot of Packard's novel offers no problem, but a supply of pine-knot torches, pickaxes, and shredded paper are indispensable kit for the tyro reader. Each of the two central characters, for example—Jimmie Dale and Marie LaSalle—has three distinct identities. Jimmie is a young millionaire bachelor, an elusive safecracker known as the Gray Seal, and a derelict hophead called Larry the Bat; Marie, likewise rich and socially élite (though forced into hiding by malefactors who crave her money), poses sometimes as the Tocsin, a shadowy fingerwoman, and again as Silver Mag, a disreputable old crone. The lives of the pair—or, more precisely, the six—are forever being sought by scores of hoodlums, gunsels, informers, shyster lawyers, and crooked shamuses, so that they are constantly compelled to switch roles. The upshot is that you are never very positive who is assaulting whom; once or twice, I got the panicky impression that Jimmie's alter egos were throttling each other. This imaginative twist, somewhat akin to the old vaudeville specialty of Desiretta, the Man Who Wrestles with Himself, proved erroneous when I checked up. It was just a couple of other felons.

Obeying the basic canon that romances about gentleman cracksmen begin in ultra-exclusive clubs, "The Adventures of Jimmie Dale" begins in one called the St. James and omits no traditional touch. Herman Carruthers, crusading young editor of the *News-Argus,* is dealing out the usual expository flapdoodle about the Gray Seal ("the kingpin of them all, the most puzzling, bewildering, delightful crook in the annals of crime") to Jimmie, who is so bland, quizzical, and mocking that even the busboys must be aware he is the marauder himself. His blandness grows practically intolerable when Carruthers avers that the kingpin is dead, for, as he and any five-year-old criminologist know, the kingpin is merely dormant until society needs his philanthropic assist. The summons reaches Jimmie that very midnight, at his luxurious Riverside Drive mansion, in the form of a note from the mysterious feminine mastermind he has never seen, who directs all his exploits. With a curious, cryptic smile tingeing his lips, Jimmie opens his safe and removes exactly what you would expect: "It was not an ordinary belt; it was full of stout-sewn, upright little pockets all the way around, and in the pockets grimly lay an array of fine, blued-steel,

highly tempered instruments—a compact, powerful burglar's kit." Half an hour later, an inconspicuous figure flits
downtown via Washington Square. Except for the black
silk mask, the slouch hat pulled well down over the eyes,
and the automatic revolver and electric flashlight, nobody
would ever suspect him of being a Raffles.

The actual caper Jimmie executes is too intricate and
inconsequential to warrant recapitulating; briefly, by leaving his telltale Gray Seal on a rifled safe, he saves from
prison a character who, in behalf of his ailing wife, has
heisted his employer's funds. A civic uproar ensues: "The
Morning *News-Argus* offered twenty-five thousand dollars
reward for the capture of the Gray Seal! Other papers
immediately followed suit in varying amounts. The authorities, State and municipal, goaded to desperation, did
likewise, and the five million men, women, and children
of New York were automatically metamorphosed into embryonic sleuths. New York was aroused." It seems odd that
such a *brouhaha* should attend a misdemeanor approximately as monstrous as spitting in the subway, but, no
doubt, Manhattan was more strait-laced in that epoch.
On the heels of the foregoing comes another sensation—
the body of a stool pigeon with alleged evidence linking
his murder to the Gray Seal. Our hero's every sensibility
is outraged: "Anger, merciless and unrestrained, surged
over Jimmie Dale. . . . Even worse to Jimmie Dale's artistic
and sensitive temperament was the vilification, the holding up to loathing, contumely, and abhorrence of the
name, the stainless name, of the Gray Seal. It *was* stainless! He had guarded it jealously—as a man guards the

woman's name he loves." Eyes flashing like cut-steel buckles, he retires to the slum hideout he calls the Sanctuary and revamps himself into Larry the Bat: "His fingers worked quickly—a little wax behind the ears, in the nostrils, under the upper lip, deftly placed—hands, wrists, neck, throat, and face received their quota of stain, applied with an artist's touch—and then the spruce, muscular Jimmie Dale, transformed into a slouching, vicious-featured denizen of the underworld, replaced the box under the flooring, pulled a slouch hat over his eyes, extinguished the gas, and went out." By dint of certain devious researches, which I could not extricate from the glue, a venal police inspector is unmasked as the culprit and the Gray Seal absolved. If my calculations are correct, Jimmie in the first sixty pages of the action has enjoyed a grand total of eleven minutes sleep, considerably less than the most wide-awake reader.

STIMULATED to a healthy glow by these finger exercises, Jimmie now dashes off an ambitious four-part fugue plangent with larceny and homicide. Under the pretense of glomming a diamond chaplet from the strongbox of a rascally broker, he recovers a note held by the Scrooge against a mining engineer he has fleeced, bilks a ring of counterfeiters blackmailing a sheep in their toils, robs a dealer of gems to obviate his being slaughtered by yeggs (a curious bit of preventive surgery), and exposes a knavish banker named Carling who has looted his own vaults and pinned the blame on an underling with a criminal record. In the last-named coup, the accused has a winsome infant, enabling Packard to pull out the *vox-humana* stop when Jimmie extorts the vital confession: "'Carling,' said Jimmie hoarsely, 'I stood beside a little bed tonight and looked at a baby girl—a little baby girl with golden hair, who smiled as she slept. . . . Take this pen, or—this.' The automatic lifted until the muzzle was on a line with Carling's eyes." Jimmie's antisocial behavior, it goes without saying, never redounds to his personal advantage; he scrupulously returns all swag to its rightful owners and, even while bashing in whatever skulls deserve it, exudes the high moral purpose of his progenitor Robin Hood. True, he betrays a pallid romantic interest in the Maid Marian who animates him from behind the scenes, but nothing that would boil an egg. In the light of contemporary pulp fiction, one marvels that Packard spiced his famous goulash with so little sexual paprika. Perhaps it may be possible to sublimate the libido by twiddling the combination of a Herring-Hall-Marvin safe, or, on the other hand, perhaps the kid's just a medical curiosity. Nobody could be *that* dedicated.

And yet he is, unless you discount the evidence of the next hundred pages. In rapid succession, he clears the reputation of a putative ruby thief, brings to book the architect of a payroll killing and his henchmen, and restores the stolen map of a gold mine to the widow and children of its legal claimant. There is a magnificent consistency about Packard's minor figures; other writers may muck about with halftones and nuances, but his widows are all destitute and enfeebled and his villains are rotten to the core. A typical sample is the satanic attorney who conceived the payroll incident above: "Cunning, shrewd, crafty, conscienceless, cold-blooded—that was Stangeist . . . the six-foot muscular frame, that was invariably clothed in attire of the most fashionable cut; the thin lips with their oily, plausible smile, the straight black hair that straggled into pinpoint, little black eyes, the dark face with its high cheekbones, which, with the pronounced aquiline nose and the persistent rumor that he was a quarter caste, had led the underworld, prejudiced always in favor of a 'monaker,' to dub the man the 'Indian Chief.'" A Choctaw version of Louis Calhern in "The Asphalt Jungle," you might say, and a real ripsnorter. The argot in which the crooks converse also has the same classical purity; *vide* that of the Weasel, an obscure cutpurse who stirs recollections of Happy Hooligan, of sainted memory: "Why, youse damned fool," jeered the Weasel, "d'youse t'ink youse can get away wid dat? Say, take it from me, youse are a piker! Say, youse make me tired. Wot d'youse t'ink youse are? D'youse t'ink dis is a tee-ayter, an' dat youse are a cheap-skate actor strollin' acrost the stage?" Scant wonder, with such nostalgic Chimmie Fadden dialogue, that youse has to swallow repeatedly to exorcise de lump in de t'roat.

THE MACHINE-GUN TEMPO, to use a flabby designation, slackens momentarily for an interview in the dark between Jimmie and the Tocsin, his female control. His work is nearing completion, she whispers, and soon she can disclose herself with impunity. This, as the intuitive will guess, is the conventional literary strip tease, because in the next breath the deluge descends. The Crime Club—not the Doubleday fellows, but "the most powerful and pitiless organization of criminals the world has ever known"—pounces on the dapper thief. In a scary milieu replete with hydraulic walls, sliding laboratories, and a binful of putty noses and false whiskers, its minions vainly ply him with a truth drug to elicit word of the Tocsin's whereabouts. No contusions result, except to the laws of English syntax, and Jimmie is let out to pasture. It would only court neuralgia to retrace the labyrinthine steps by which the author maneuvers him into the arms of his lady, now disguised as Silver Mag, the beggarwoman, but ultimately the lovebirds make contact and the lava spills over: "The warm, rich lips were yielding to his; he could feel that throb, the life in the young, lithe form against his own. She was his—his! The years, the past, all were swept away—and she was his at last—his for always. And there came a mighty sense of kingship upon him, as though all the world were at his feet, and virility, and a great, glad strength above all other men's, and a song was in his soul, a song triumphant—for she was his!" In other words, she was his, *Gott sei dank*, and you have just burst into sobs of relief when the whole confounded business begins over again. Marie LaSalle, alias the Tocsin, alias Silver Mag, pours out a long, garbled *histoire*, the kernel of which is that the head of the Crime Club, posing as her uncle, seeks to kill her for her estate. Jimmie manages to worm a confession from him clinching his guilt; in the attendant melee, though, he is recognized as the Gray Seal, and a wrathful mob of vigilantes from the Tenderloin tracks him to the Sanctuary and puts it to the torch. The lovers providentially escape over the rooftops to continue their didos in "The Further Adventures of Jimmie Dale," "Jimmie Dale and the Phantom Clue," and "Jimmie Dale and the Blue Envelope," and blessed silence descends, broken only by the scratch of Packard's pen endorsing his royalty checks.

I was in a Sixth Avenue bus, traffic-bound in Herald Square, when I finished the last three chapters, and a natural impulse to break clean made me drop the book into the vacant seat before me. Moments later, a brace of speedy sixteen-year-olds in windbreakers emblazoned with side elevations of Jane Russell crash-dived into the seat and buried themselves in comics. One of them suddenly detected the volume nestling against his spine. "Hey!" he exclaimed. "Someone lost a book." "It ain't a book. There's no pictures in it," his companion corrected. Together they laboriously spelled out the title and joined in a quick, incurious survey of the contents. "Ah, just a lot of slush," observed the first, in disdain. "What kind of an old creep'd get a charge out of this stuff?" An old creep directly behind them turned blush-pink, fastened his eyes on a Mojud stocking ad, and strove to retain his dignity. At Forty-second Street, weary of their tiresome speculation and

guffaws, he disembarked, not, however, without a shrivel-
ling glance. If you ask me, popinjays like that, and all
these young whippersnappers you meet nowadays, have
no more character than a tin pie plate. Why, at their age
I was already chairman of a world-famed debating society.

Young as You Feel

⊂⊃

If there is one thing in the world calculated to throw a man in his mid-forties on his beam-ends, to yank the rug from under his self-esteem, shrivel his ego to the size of a chick-pea, and emboss his forehead with ice-cold, king's-size drops of perspiration, it is a tailor's mirror. Strictly speaking, a tailor's mirror is not a looking-glass at all; it is a machine-age version of the pillory, a peep into total annihilation, a view of your psyche with its suspenders down. Employing one of the sneakiest principles in physics, the law of triple reflection, it is designed to show you facets of yourself you never dreamed existed. The scales suddenly fall from your eyes and you gaze stricken on those vast uncharted areas, mercifully hidden over the years, which your enemies see constantly. The hawklike profile you have always secretly considered as combining the spirituality of St. Francis with the dash of a Mississippi River gambler abruptly turns out to resemble a sheep's; the neck would seem sensual even in a butcher. In the background stands the clothing salesman or fitter, pretending to be detached but actually feasting on your humiliation. You read in his opaque eyes the conviction that you are a poltroon and a blatherskite, and yet you are powerless to refute it. It is a horrible moment.

It was about four months ago that I last let myself be inveigled into the ordeal by mirror, and it was proving the Waterloo I had anticipated. The chalk-stripe gray suit I had selected was the exact duplicate of the habit I had always worn, but brownies had mysteriously made free with it. A bulge like a Rocky Ford melon protruded just north of the paunch, the three top vest-buttons were not even within kissing distance of the holes, and the hindquarters were strained as tight as a spinnaker under a southwest breeze. The hangdog character gaping back at me was nobody I remembered having seen before; he could have passed for some small-time hoodlum picked up in a poolroom raid.

"Not bad," commented the salesman, cocking his head judiciously. "It's very youthful."

"What do you mean, youthful?" I said, flaring up. "I can get around all right without the aid of a cane."

"Sure you can," he said soothingly. "It's a long time

237

before they'll be making glue out of you, as the fellow said."

"Never mind the folk wisdom," I snapped. "I've been trading here twenty-five years and I've never seen such a shocking fit."

"Ah—er—possibly you've put on a pound or so since your last visit," he said with a discreet cough. "You know how it is when a man of your age stops exercising—and then those sweets between meals—"

"Look, friend," I said, exhibiting my doubled fist. "It may interest you to learn that I can still drive a spike through an oak plank with this."

"They're using hammers for that type of work nowadays," he returned. "Hold still while I rip the waistband, will you, old-timer?" The epithet rankled all afternoon, and despite the banana split with which I tried to assuage my lacerated feelings, I kept brooding over it. Clearly there was some sort of whispering campaign in motion, aimed to remove me from the running by implying that I was a dotard. A little group of men in high places had decided that I knew too much, that my lips must be sealed at all costs. Instinct told me that they would stick at nothing and that their agents were probably watching me at that very moment, poised to strike. Sure enough; as I cast a veiled glance around the soda fountain, the dispenser smoothly removed the remainder of my split and laid down a check.

"You don't need the rest of that, Dad," he said, a crooked smile contorting his mouth. "I'd watch my weight if I was in your shoes." It was neatly done, and to anyone unaware of the conspiracy, might have seemed insignificant, but it corroborated my suspicions. Instantly my every faculty was on the *qui vive*. So that was their game, was it? Well, I'd show them what sort of opponent they were up against. The battle was joined.

The first skirmish took place, unromantically enough, in the onion bed at my country place a fortnight later, as I was superintending the preparation of the soil by two young week-end guests. Vivacious and well-knit lassies both, dancers out of a Broadway musical show, they had joyously hailed my suggestion that they dig up the patch as a means of keeping their muscles in condition. It was, frankly, a tiresome chore for me, for it involved dragging the considerable gear I needed all the way out to the garden—a cumbrous deck chair, megaphone, soda, ice, sun-tan lotion (I burn quite easily) and the like. Anyway, I gave freely of my strength without demur, and dehydrating profusely, lay back calling out advice and encouragement to the pair. Quite by accident, I became conscious that they were eyeing me critically, spades akimbo.

"Look at that slug, will you?" panted one under her breath. "At least he might *offer* to help us shovel."

"Too old," said the other. "He hasn't lifted anything heavier than a Sazerac since he put on long pants."

A hot tide of resentment welled up within me. I felt a wild impulse to wrest the tools from them and demonstrate what I was capable of if sufficiently provoked, but I knew better than to give way to passing anger. When

239

all but the last couple of rows were dug and the girls lay gasping on the grass, I judged the proper psychological moment had come. Picking up a spade, I spat on my hands, squared my jaw, and fell grimly to work. How the clods flew, as, like some mighty, tireless engine, I churned up the fertile loam; in less time than it would have taken Millet to paint "The Gleaners," the task was complete. Out of the corner of my eye, I saw that feminine sneers had yielded to startled admiration, but I was not one to crow over a defeated adversary. I sucked in my fluttering stomach, winked away the rain of black specks fogging my vision, and strode into the house, where I stayed in bed the next four days. The doctor told me subsequently that I had contracted a virus from drinking contaminated seltzer, and right or wrong, I prefer the opinion of an accredited medical man to that of some beat-out Broadway showgirls.

NEWS must have trickled through to the proper quarters that it had been a mistake to underestimate my potentialities, because no effort was made for a while to goad me into displaying them. Then, one gusty April afternoon, another challenge flashed out of the blue. I was helping my wife and children clean out the leaves that had collected in the gutters over the winter. The problem of steadying the ladder against the porch, so as to provide the woman with reasonably safe footing, was the most ticklish phase of the operation, but thanks to my uncanny sense of balance, she was as safe as though she were in an oxygen tent, and the work was proceeding apace. All of a sudden, however, she was summoned to the phone by a long-distance call from Lisbon—actually, I realize now, a clever ruse schemed up by the cabal to force my hand.

"Up you go, Junior," I directed my eleven-year-old son, fired by a bright inspiration. "Let's surprise Mummy and finish before she gets back."

"You surprise her," he said sullenly. "I got enough trouble without a plaster cast."

"Scared, eh?" I jeered. "Listen, I'm roughly four times your age—"

"And four times as yellow," his younger sister finished. "Never mind—I'll go."

"Oh, so you think I'm just an old has-been, do you?" I choked. "Well, you've got another think coming." With a bound, I sprang up the ladder, and hooking a knee through the top rung, lunged at the leaves. "Watch this, wise guys!" I shouted. I was so full of elation at my feat that I did not hear the warning cries below. As the ladder swung sickeningly outward, there was just time to grab hold of the gutter and hang suspended until aid arrived. The four-foot drop might have snapped my ankles like pipe-stems, but fortunately, my cries were audible to our neighboring farmer half a mile away. While trifling, the incident was widely discussed in the community, and I could tell from the hush that befell the general store when I entered that my dauntlessness had borne fruit.

The Ill-Tempered Clavichord

THE STROKE that really sent my traducers slithering into
their holes, though, and forever extracted their venom,
was dealt them the night of my twenty-fifth college reunion. Between ourselves, I had been reluctant to attend,
suspecting that the sight of a jaunty figure and hair as
black as the raven's wing would shame my doddering
classmates, but I weakly gave in when they persuaded me
to appear, if only for contrast. Notwithstanding, I thought
as I entered the ballroom where our silver jubilee dance
was in progress that I had blundered into some ghostly
quadrille. These decrepit, shrunken gaffers waltzing staidly
about, with their wigs askew and dentures flapping—could
they be the youths I had rollicked with in the Jazz Age?
My worst misgivings were justified; one after the other,
seamed faces nodded welcome and called out greetings in
voices that croaked like Aristophanes' *Frogs*. Just as I was
deciding to steal away to some milieu on my own age
level, say a Fifty-second Street jam session, an elderly
fogy clapped me boisterously on the back.

"Didn't recognize you, Skinny," he quavered. "You're
as flabby as those old quilts we used when we roomed together." I shook hands distantly and remarked that, unlike
his, my teeth were still first editions.

"They look it," he chuckled, presenting the young lady
with him and vanishing into the bar. For some reason I
could not fathom, unless that she noticed my fleeting resemblance to Vernon Castle, the creature began pressing

me to dance with her. I declined gracefully, explaining that I gave only charity exhibitions now, but she deliberately chose to misunderstand.

"I know—it's the arteries," she said. "Wait a minute, Pops—I'll find you a chair." My blood boiled up at the injustice of the slur; an instant later, we were circling the floor dizzily, pirouetting and dipping like swallows, our bodies moving as two to the savage beat of the music. The other dancers, electrified by skill they could not hope to rival, gave ground and applauded us on; the orchestra quickened its rhythm to match our flying feet. Around and round we went, shifting from the Cubanola glide into the toddle, from the bunny hug to the maxixe and the balconade. The saxophones were sobbing "La Veeda, Maid of Spain," and I was whirling my breathless partner through the intricacies of the camel walk when I noticed to my consternation that she had developed two heads and that steam was issuing from both. Simultaneously, a factory whistle deep in my thyroid gave a long, piercing blast to signalize the close of business, and before I could claw open my collar to equalize the pressure, I was a forty-six-year-old alumnus entirely surrounded by floor.

Well, men, say what you will, there's nothing like a few weeks on the horizontal to tone up the system. You catch up on your reading and you get plenty of exercise, too, slamming down the phone when your friends call up to commiserate. Just for the record, I feel right as rain, fine as silk, and sound as a nut, and the moment the doc gives me the nod, I figure to get down to the seashore for a nice rest. Some place without too many young flibbertigibbets cavorting about and raising Cain till all hours. I love young people, but they're so darn *shallow*. You never know what they're thinking—and maybe it's just as well.